Instant Pot Pressure Cooker Cookbook #2019

600 Deliciously Simple Recipes for Beginners and Advanced Users

Maria Dominguez

Description 5

Introduction 5

Breakfast 6
    Lemon Steel Cut Oats 6
    Cranberry Farro 6
    Strawberries Oatmeal 6
    Peaches Oatmeal 7
    Egg Casserole 7
    Quinoa Bowls 8
    Mushrooms and Sausage Mix 8
    Blackberries Pancake 9
    French Eggs 9
    Buckwheat Porridge 9
    Zucchini Muffins 10
    Burrito Bowls 10
    Kale Muffins 11
    Peach Oatmeal 11
    Instant Nutritious Porridge 12
    Coco Rice Pudding 12
    Old Fashioned Butter Oatmeal 13
    Cinnamon Quinoa 13
    Pineapple Oatmeal 14
    Special Red Beans Casserole 14

Side dish 15
    Zucchini Rice 15
    Spiced Carrot Rice 15
    Herbed Mash 16
    Currant Rice 16
    Mint Farro Side Salad 17
    Lemon Spinach Rice 17
    Cheesy Thyme Rice 18
    Greek Potato Mix 18
    Squash and Potato Mash 19
    Cinnamon Potatoes 19
    Potato and Parsnip Wedges 20
    Balsamic Green Beans 20
    Quinoa Cucumber Salad 21
    Lovely Lime Potatoes 21
    Mashed Potatoes 22
    Mac and Cheese 22
    Easy Maple Glazed Brussel Sprouts 23
    Garlic with Beets 23
    Cabbage and Bacon 24
    Dijon White Beans 24
    Baked Potato 25
    Spiced Potatoes 25

    Creamy Turnips Potato Mash 26
    Potato Pumpkin Mash 26
    Dill Butter Potato 27

Chicken & Poultry 27
    Chicken and Peppercorns 27
    Turkey and Tomato Sauce 27
    Ginger Turkey and Potatoes 28
    Turkey and Carrots Mix 28
    Creamy Turkey 29
    Sage Turkey and Sweet Potatoes 29
    Chicken and Ginger Asparagus 30
    Balsamic Chicken 30
    Turkey and Ginger Rice 31
    Rosemary Chicken and Green Beans 31
    Scampi Chicken 32
    Turkey Breasts with Basil and Tomato Sauce . 32
    Special Chicken Masala 33
    Turkey and Smoked Paprika 34
    Chicken with Lime Juice 34
    Amazing Turkey Stuffed Tacos 35
    Juicy Chicken Tacos 36

Beef, lamb & pork 36
    Beef and Artichokes 36
    Lemony Beef Mix 37
    Beef and Shallots Sauce 37
    Cheesy Beef and Carrots 38
    Beef and Zucchini Mix 38
    Cinnamon Beef and Asparagus 39
    Beef and Red Cabbage Mix 39
    Cheesy Lamb 40
    Sage Lamb Ribs 40
    Herbed Lamb Shanks 41
    Pork Chops and Apples 41
    Pork and Parsley Sauce 42
    Tomato Pork Chops 42
    Pork and Endives 43
    Sesame Pork Chops 43
    Pork and Fennel 44
    Mexican Butter Beef Recipe 44
    Mushroom Beef Stroganoff 45
    Lamb Curry Recipe 45
    Beef and Bacon Casserole 46
    Special Lamb Stew 46
    Amazing Lamb Chops 47
    Jamaican Pork Roast Recipe 48
    Pork Sausages and Mushrooms 48

Instant Bacon Lamb Chili 49
Quick Spicy Minced Meat 49
Spicy Pork Ribs 50

Fish & seafood 51
Shrimp and Parsley Mix 51
Cod and Cauliflower Rice 51
Salmon And Baby Carrots 51
Spicy Trout 52
Thyme Cod and Tomatoes 52
Salmon Cakes and Sauce 53
Sea Bass and Artichokes 53
Cod and Strawberries Sauce 54
Tilapia and Lemon Sauce 54
Shrimp and Chicken Mix 55
Tuna and Tomatoes 55
Simple Fish Tacos 56
Balsamic Salmon 56
Shrimp Gumbo 57
Quick Garlic Mussels 57
Shrimp Risotto 58
Basil Tomato Tilapia 58
Shrimp Herb Risotto 59
Tuna Cheese Noodles 59

Soup & Stews 60
Ginger Cod Soup 60
Potato and Parsley Cream 60
Corn and Zucchini Soup 61
Bell Pepper and Tomato Soup 61
Carrots and Cabbage Soup 62
Salsa Turkey Soup 62
Tarragon Corn Soup 63
Zucchini and Chicken Soup 63
Bacon Corn Soup 64
Chicken and Pea Soup 64
Beef and Tomato Soup 65
Chicken and Eggplant Soup 65
Turmeric Kale Stew 66
Zucchini and Cabbage Stew 66
Chicken and Cranberries Stew 67
Mushroom and Carrots Stew 67
Artichokes and Beef Stew 68
Greek Lamb Stew 68
Lamb and Green Beans Stew 68

Beans, Grains, Rice & pasta 69
Flavorful Italian Black Beans 69
Sweet Maple Baked Beans 70
Flavors Chipotle Black Beans 71
Beans with Tomatillos 71
Delicious Beans with Bacon 72
Healthy Vegetable Quinoa 73
Quinoa with Sausage 73
Chicken Salsa Brown Rice 74
Jalapeno Tomato Brown Rice 74
Easy Butter Rice 75
Tasty Potato Risotto 75
Garlic Bean Rice 76
Butter Paprika Rice 76
Salsa Rice 77
Parmesan Butter Risotto 78
Squash Mushroom Risotto 78
Parsley Scallions Risotto 79
Cauliflower Risotto 79
Cauliflower Turmeric Rice 80
Coconut Cauliflower Rice 80
Spaghetti Noodles 81
Polenta with Grape Tomatoes 81
Simple Pearl Barley 82
Lemon Dill Couscous 82
Butter Brown Rice 82
Vegetable Pesto Quinoa 83
Garlic Lima Beans 83
Hearty White Beans with Tomato 84
Garlic Garbanzo Beans 84
Classic Wild Rice 85

Vegetables 85
Crockpot Pumpkin Chili 85
Vegan Pulled "Pork" 86
Instant Pot Cajun Peanuts 86
Indian Coconut Kale Curry 86
Veggie Cheese Soup 87
Instant Pot Zucchini Casserole 87
Creamy Artichoke, Garlic, And Zucchini 88
Crockpot Summer Veggies Side Dish 88
Instant Pot Basic Steamed Vegetables 89
Instant Pot French Onion Soup 89
Steamed Vegetables Side Dish 90
Hummus Under Pressure 90
Big Potatoes and Peas Bowl 91
Collard Greens Refined Hummus 91
Saucy BBQ Veggie Meal 92
Vegan Swiss Chard Dip 92
Cheesy Asparagus and Spinach Dip 92
Classic Easy Italian Peperonata 93

Spicy Tomato Sauce 93

Appetizers 94
    Chives Salmon Bites 94
    Eggplant Salad... 94
    Basil Shrimp Salad 95
    Spinach Dip 95
    Mint Spinach and Shrimp Salad.................... 95
    Red Beans Spread 96
    Cod Salad 96
    Pesto Shrimp and Tomato Salad.................... 97
    Chicken and Peppers Salad 97
    Mussels and Spinach Bowls 98
    Tomato Salsa 98
    Hot Mussels Salad... 99
    Turkey Salad 99
    Silician Meat Sauce 100
    Cranberry Pecan Brie 101
    Tavern Burgers.. 101

Dessert 102
    Mini Lemon Cheesecakes............................. 102
    Chocolate Layered Coconut Cups 102
    Pumpkin Pie Chocolate Cups 103
    Fudgy Cake... 103
    Peppermint Patties 105
    Buttery Pecan Delights 105
    Squash and Carrots Pudding........................ 105

Tapioca and Quinoa Pudding 106
Indian Rice Pudding 106
Coconut Cake... 107
Brown Rice Pudding...................................... 107
Egg Custard.. 108
Sweet Potato Pudding 108
Coconut Custard 109
Creamy Pecan Pudding................................. 109
Pumpkin Pudding... 110
Almond and Apples Bowls 110
Coconut Grapes Cream................................. 110
Orange Cream 111
Egg Pudding.. 111
Cinnamon Apples juice 112
Lime Pear Bowls... 112
Apple and Cauliflower Rice Pudding............. 113
Delightful Fruity Custard............................... 113
Sweet Honey Yogurt Recipe......................... 114
IP Brown Fudge Cake 114
Awesome Apple Bread Pudding 115
Walnut Carrot Cake 115
Instant Chocolate Crème Brûlée 116
Awesome Wine Glazed Apples 117
Yummy Apple Custard Trifle 117
Almond Cheese-cake 118

Conclusion 119

Description

An instant pot is one of the kitchen devices you can't do without in this fast-changing world of technology! It just doesn't make your life in the kitchen easy, but also prepares you delicious meals quickly. But wait! What can you do with it if you have no idea of what meals to prepare? Well, this book has been written to help you prepare the mouth-watering meals that will also help you watch your weight as you devour the delicacies.

The recipes in this book are my favorite, they make every minute spent in the kitchen worth!

You are certainly covered from being able to prepare:

- breakfast
- lunch
- side dishes
- pork and beef
- chicken and poultry
- fish and seafood
- vegetarian dishes
- dessert

Hopefully, the recipes in this book will be a great starting point for you!
Happy Cooking!

Introduction

This book is an amazing collection of instant pot recipes that are so unique and delicious! You've never had the chance to enjoy such a cooking journal before!

Cooking in your instant pot is so much easier now that you have this special cookbook at hand!

You will end up loving your instant pot and cooking with it once you discover these great weight watching recipes here.

So, what are you waiting for? Grab this copy and get set to begin making the most out of your instant pot and to put a smile on your family's face!

Breakfast

Lemon Steel Cut Oats

Preparation time: 10 minutes
Cooking time: 13 minutes
Serves: 4
Ingredients:
- 1 cup steel cut oats
- 3 cups water
- ½ cup coconut cream
- 1 tablespoon avocado oil
- 2 tablespoons coconut sugar
- 1 tablespoon lemon zest, grated
- ¼ cup chia seeds
- 1 cup blueberries

Directions:
1. Set the instant pot on Sauté mode, add the oil, heat it up, add the oats and toast them for 3 minutes.
2. Add all the other ingredients except the chia seeds and blueberries, toss, put the lid on and cook on High for 10 minutes.
3. Release he pressure naturally for 10 minutes, add chia seeds and blueberries and mix everything.
4. Divide into bowls and serve for breakfast.

Nutrition Value: calories 182, fat 10, fiber 5, carbs 8, protein 8

Cranberry Farro

Preparation time: 10 minutes
Cooking time: 20 minutes
Serves: 4
Ingredients:
- 16 ounces farro
- ½ cup brown sugar
- 4 and ½ cups water
- 1 teaspoon lemon extract
- ½ cup cranberries

Directions:
1. In your instant pot, combine all the ingredients, toss, put the lid on and cook on High for 20 minutes.
2. Release the pressure naturally for 10 minutes, divide the mix into bowls and serve for breakfast.

Nutrition Value: calories 165, fat 5, fiber 5, carbs 7, protein 10

Strawberries Oatmeal

Preparation time: 20 minutes
Cooking time: 13 minutes
Serves: 4
Ingredients:
- 1 tablespoon avocado oil
- 1 cup steel cut oats
- ¼ cup heavy cream

- 4 cups water
- ¼ cup chia seeds
- 1 and ½ cups strawberries, sliced
- 3 tablespoons coconut sugar

Directions:
1. Set the instant pot on Sauté mode, add the oil, heat it up, add the oats and toast them for 3 minutes.
2. Add the rest of the ingredients except the chia seeds and strawberries, put the lid on and cook on High for 10 minutes.
3. Release the pressure naturally for 10 minutes, add the strawberries and the chia seeds and toss.
4. Leave everything aside for 10 minutes more, divide into bowls and serve for breakfast.

Nutrition Value: calories 188, fat 6, fiber 4, carbs 6, protein 9

Peaches Oatmeal

Preparation time: 10 minutes
Cooking time: 4 minutes
Serves: 4

Ingredients:
- 4 cups water
- 1 peach, stone removed and chopped
- 1 teaspoon vanilla extract
- 2 cups rolled oats
- ½ cup almonds, chopped
- 2 tablespoons flax meal

Directions:
1. In your instant pot, combine the oats with water, peach, and the vanilla, put the lid on and cook on High for 3 minutes.
2. Release the pressure naturally for 10 minutes, add the almonds and flax meal, toss, divide into bowls and serve for breakfast.

Nutrition Value: calories 171, fat 8, fiber 4, carbs 6, protein 5

Egg Casserole

Preparation time: 10 minutes
Cooking time: 20 minutes
Serves: 6

Ingredients:
- 32 ounces hash browns
- 2 cups turkey sausage, casings removed and ground
- 1 yellow onion, chopped
- 2 cups cheddar cheese, shredded
- 12 eggs, whisked
- 1 cup coconut milk
- A pinch of salt and black pepper
- Cooking spray

Directions:
1. Grease the instant pot with cooking spray and spread the hash browns, onion and turkey sausage on the bottom.
2. In a bowl, mix the eggs with the rest of the ingredients, whisk and pour over the hash browns.
3. Put the lid on and cook on High for 20 minutes.
4. Release the pressure naturally for 10 minutes, divide into bowls and serve for breakfast.

Nutrition Value: calories 200, fat 8, fiber 4, carbs 6, protein 8

Quinoa Bowls

Preparation time: 10 minutes
Cooking time: 1 minute
Serves: 6

Ingredients:
- 1 and ½ cups quinoa
- 14 ounces coconut milk
- 1 and ½ cups water
- 2 tablespoons coconut sugar
- 2 teaspoons vanilla extract
- 1 teaspoon cinnamon powder
- 2 apples, cored and cubed

Directions:
1. In your instant pot, combine all the ingredients except the apples, toss, put the lid on and cook on High for 1 minute.
2. Release the pressure naturally for 10 minutes, stir the quinoa, divide into bowls, sprinkle the apples on top and serve.

Nutrition Value: calories 200, fat 8, fiber 5, carbs 6, protein 10

Mushrooms and Sausage Mix

Preparation time: 10 minutes
Cooking time: 30 minutes
Serves: 6

Ingredients:
- 2 cups almond milk
- 12 eggs, whisked
- ½ cup cheddar cheese, grated
- ½ cup feta cheese, crumbled
- A pinch of salt and black pepper
- 1 pound pork sausage, casings removed and chopped
- 2 cups spinach, chopped
- 1 cup red onion, chopped
- 1 cup white mushrooms, sliced
- 1 tablespoon olive oil

Directions:
1. Set the instant pot on Sauté mode, add the oil, heat it up, add the onion, stir and sauté for 3 minutes.
2. Add the sausage, toss and brown for 2 minutes more.
3. Add the mushrooms and the spinach, stir and brown for another 3 minutes.
4. Add the eggs whisked with the milk, salt and pepper and spread.
5. Sprinkle the cheddar and the feta cheese, put the lid on and cook on High for 20 minutes.
6. Release the pressure naturally for 10 minutes, divide the mix between plates and serve for breakfast.

Nutrition Value: calories 200, fat 12, fiber 6, carbs 7, protein 9

Blackberries Pancake

Preparation time: 5 minutes
Cooking time: 15 minutes
Serves: 4

Ingredients:
- 2 cups almond flour
- 2 teaspoons baking powder
- 1 teaspoon baking soda
- ¼ cup coconut sugar
- 2 eggs, whisked
- 1 and ½ cups almond milk
- 1 cup blackberries
- Cooking spray

Directions:
1. In a bowl, combine gradually all the ingredients except the cooking spray and whisk well.
2. Grease the instant pot with the cooking spray, pour the pancake mix and spread well into the pot.
3. Put the lid on and cook on High for 15 minutes.
4. Release the pressure fast for 5 minutes, divide the pancake between plates and serve for breakfast.

Nutrition Value: calories 170, fat 10, fiber 4, carbs 7, protein 9

French Eggs

Preparation time: 10 minutes
Cooking time: 2 minutes
Serves: 4

Ingredients:
- Cooking spray
- 2 tablespoons chives, chopped
- 4 eggs
- 4 tablespoons heavy cream
- A pinch of salt and black pepper
- 1 cup water

Directions:
1. Grease 4 ramekins with cooking spray and divide the cream in each.
2. Crack an egg in each ramekin, sprinkle with salt, pepper and the chives.
3. Put the water in the instant pot, add the trivet inside, add the ramekins in the pot, put the lid on and cook on High for 2 minutes.
4. Release the pressure naturally for 10 minutes, and serve the eggs for breakfast.

Nutrition Value: calories 181, fat 11, fiber 2, carbs 6, protein 9

Buckwheat Porridge

Preparation time: 20 minutes
Cooking time: 6 minutes
Serves: 4

Ingredients:

- 1 cup buckwheat
- ¼ cup raisins
- 3 cups almond milk
- 1 banana, peeled and sliced
- ½ teaspoon vanilla extract
- 1 teaspoon cinnamon powder

Directions:
1. In your instant pot, combine all the ingredients, put the lid on and cook on High for 6 minutes.
2. Release the pressure naturally for 20 minutes, divide the porridge into bowls and serve for breakfast.

Nutrition Value: calories 172, fat 8, fiber 2, carbs 7, protein 9

Zucchini Muffins

Preparation time: 10 minutes
Cooking time: 8 minutes
Serves: 4

Ingredients:
- 2 eggs, whisked
- 1 cup coconut milk
- ½ cup avocado oil
- 2 teaspoons vanilla extract
- 3 tablespoons cocoa powder
- 1 cup almond flour
- 1 teaspoon cinnamon powder
- ½ teaspoon baking soda
- 1 cup zucchinis, grated
- 1 cup water
- 1/3 chocolate chips
- Cooking spray

Directions:
1. In a bowl, combine all the ingredients except the cooking spray and stir well.
2. Divide this into 8 muffin tins.
3. Put the racket in the pot, put the muffin tins inside, put the lid on and cook on High for 8 minutes.
4. Release the pressure naturally for 10 minutes, divide the muffins between plates and serve for breakfast.

Nutrition Value: calories 188, fat 11, fiber 6, carbs 9, protein 7

Burrito Bowls

Preparation time: 10 minutes
Cooking time: 7 minutes
Serves: 4

Ingredients:
- 3 tablespoons olive oil
- 6 eggs, whisked
- A pinch of salt and black pepper

- ½ pound pork sausage, cooked and crumbled
- ½ cup mild salsa
- ½ cup cheddar cheese, shredded
- ½ cup sour cream
- 1 avocado, peeled, pitted and cubed
- ¼ cup green onions, chopped

Directions:
1. Set the instant pot on Sauté mode, add the oil, heat it up, add the eggs, salt and pepper, and stir.
2. Add the sausage, toss, put the lid on and cook on High for 7 minutes.
3. Release the pressure naturally for 10 minutes, divide the mix into bowls, top each serving with cheese, salsa, sour cream, avocado and green onions and serve.

Nutrition Value: calories 200, fat 8, fiber 5, carbs 7, protein 11

Kale Muffins

Preparation time: 10 minutes
Cooking time: 10 minutes
Serves: 2

Ingredients:
- 4 ounces chicken sausage, cooked and chopped
- 3 teaspoons avocado oil
- 4 kale leaves, chopped
- 4 eggs, whisked
- A pinch of salt and black pepper
- ¼ cup coconut milk
- 4 tablespoons cheddar cheese, shredded
- 1 cup water

Directions:
1. Grease 4 muffin tins with 1 teaspoon oil and leave them aside for now.
2. Set the instant pot on sauté mode, add the rest of the oil, heat it up, add the sausage and brown for 2 minutes.
3. Add kale, salt and pepper, stir and cook for 2 minutes.
4. In a bowl, combine the eggs with coconut milk, salt and pepper and whisk.
5. Add sausage and kale mix, stir and divide evenly into the muffin tins.
6. Clean the pot, add the water, add the trivet inside and arrange the muffin tin in the pot.
7. Put the lid on, and cook on High for 5 minutes.
8. Release the pressure for 10 minutes and serve the muffins for breakfast.

Nutrition Value: Calories 200, fat 12, fiber 5, carbs 6, protein 8

Peach Oatmeal

Preparation Time: 11 minutes
Serves: 4
Nutrition Values
- Calories:- 458
- Carbohydrate:- 80.2g
- Protein:- 15.2g
- Fat:- 8.2g
- Sugar:- 27.8g
- Sodium:- 0.35 g

Ingredients
- 2 peaches; peeled and sliced

- 2 cups old-fashioned oats
- 2 ¼ cups water
- 2 ¼ cups milk
- 1/2 tsp. salt
- 1/2 tsp. ground cinnamon
- 1/4 cup sugar

Directions:
1. Add all the Ingredients to Instant Pot. Save a few peach slices for garnishing.
2. Secure the lid of instant pot and press *Multigrain option.*
3. Adjust the time to 6 minutes and let it cook.
4. After it beeps; release the pressure naturally and remove the lid. Serve with peach slices on top

Instant Nutritious Porridge

Preparation Time: 8 minutes
Serves: 4
Nutrition Values
- Calories:- 615
- Carbohydrate:- 29.4g
- Protein:- 14.9g
- Fat:- 53.4g
- Sugar:- 9.5g
- Sodium:- 24mg

Ingredients
- 1 cup cashews (raw, unsalted
- 1/2 cup Pepitas; shelled
- 1 cup Pecan halves
- 4 tsp. coconut oil; melted
- 2 tbsp. maple syrup or honey
- 1 cup unsweetened dried coconut shreds
- 2 cups water

Directions:
1. Add all the Ingredients to a blender, except water, maple syrup and coconut oil. Blend well to form a smooth mixture,
2. Add the prepared mixture along with water, coconut oil and maple syrup to Instant Pot.
3. Secure the lid of instant pot and press *Porridge* option.
4. Adjust the time to 3 minutes and let it cook.
5. When it beeps; release the pressure naturally and remove the lid.
6. Stir the prepared mixture and serve in a bowl. Garnish with fresh fruits and cashews on top.

Coco Rice Pudding

Preparation Time: 15 minutes
Serves: 2
Nutrition Values
- Calories:- 476
- Carbohydrate:- 36.5g
- Protein:- 18.6g
- Fat:- 27.9g
- Sugar:- 9.8g
- Sodium:- 0.88g

Ingredients
- 1/2 cup basmati rice; short grain

- 1 cup coconut milk
- Whipped cream and coconut flakes (garnish
- 3/4 cup water
- 1/2 cup coconut cream
- 2 tbsp. maple syrup
- Pinch of sea salt

Directions:
1. Add all the Ingredients to Instant Pot.
2. Secure the lid of instant pot and press *Manual* function key.
3. Adjust the time to 10 minutes and cook at high pressure,
4. After it beeps; release the pressure naturally and remove the lid.
5. Stir the prepared pudding and serve in a bowl. Add whipped cream and coconut flakes on top.

Old Fashioned Butter Oatmeal

Preparation Time: 11 minutes
Serves: 4
Nutrition Values
- Calories:- 512
- Carbohydrate:- 73.3g
- Protein:- 18.8g
- Fat:- 16g
- Sugar:- 18.6g
- Sodium:- 0.144g

Ingredients
- 2 cups old-fashioned oats
- 2 ¼ cups water
- 1 tbsp. sugar
- 4 tbsp. peanut butter
- 2 ¼ cups milk
- 1/4 cup dry fruits

Directions:
1. Add all the ingredients; except for dry fruits, to Instant Pot.
2. Secure the lid of instant pot and press *Manual* function key.
3. Adjust the time to 6 minutes and cook at high pressure,
4. When it beeps; release the pressure naturally and remove the lid.
5. Stir the prepared oatmeal and serve in a bowl. Garnish with dry fruits on top.

Cinnamon Quinoa

Preparation Time: 17 minutes
Serves: 3
Nutrition Values
- Calories:- 370
- Carbohydrate:- 40.9g
- Protein:- 7.8g
- Fat:- 20.6g
- Sugar:- 10.7g
- Sodium:- 18mg

Ingredients
- 3/4 cup quinoa; soaked in water at least 1 hour
- 1/2 tsp. ground cinnamon
- 1 (8 oz. can coconut milk
- 3/4 cup water

- 2 tbsp. pure maple syrup
- 1 tsp. vanilla extract
- 1 pinch of salt

Toppings:
- Fresh fruits
- Coconut flakes

Directions:
1. Add all the Ingredients for quinoa to Instant Pot.
2. Secure the lid of instant pot and press *Rice* option.
3. Adjust the time to 12 minutes and cook at low pressure,
4. When it beeps; release the pressure naturally and remove the lid.
5. Stir the prepared quinoa well and serve in a bowl. Add fresh fruits and coconut flakes on top. Add more milk if needed.

Pineapple Oatmeal

Preparation Time: 11 minutes
Serves: 4
Nutrition Values
- Calories:- 434
- Carbohydrate:- 73.7g
- Protein:- 15g
- Fat:- 8.1g
- Sugar:- 16.4g
- Sodium:- 73mg

Ingredients
- 2 cups pineapple; chopped.
- 2 cups old-fashioned oats
- 2 ¼ cups water
- 2 ¼ cups milk
- 1 tbsp. cinnamon sugar
- 2 tbsp. fresh mint leaves

Directions:
1. Add oats, milk, water and cinnamon sugar in the Instant Pot.
2. Secure the lid of instant pot and press *Manual* function key.
3. Adjust the time to 6 minutes and cook at high pressure,
4. When it beeps; release the pressure naturally and remove the lid.
5. Stir the prepared oatmeal. Serve with fresh mint leaves and pineapple on top.

Special Red Beans Casserole

Preparation Time: 25 minutes
Serves: 3
Nutrition Values
- Calories:- 318
- Carbohydrate:- 21.6g
- Protein:- 21.2g
- Fat:- 16.6g
- Sugar:- 1.6g
- Sodium:- 0.48g

Ingredients
- 1/2 cup red beans; boiled
- 3 eggs

- 1/2 small onion chopped
- 1/2 cup cooked ham or bacon
- 1/4 cup heavy cream
- 1/2 cup cheddar cheese
- Sea salt and pepper; to taste

Directions:
1. Add 1 cup water to Instant Pot and place the trivet inside,
2. Add all the Ingredients to a bowl except cheese and whisk well.
3. Take a heatproof container and pour the egg mixture into it.
4. Place the container over the trivet.
5. Secure the lid of instant pot and press *Manual* function key.
6. Adjust the time to 20 minutes and cook at high pressure,
7. When it beeps; release the pressure naturally and remove the lid. Drizzle the shredded cheese on top and serve hot.

Side dish

Zucchini Rice

Preparation time: 5 minutes
Cooking time: 15 minutes
Serves: 4

Ingredients:
- 2 tablespoons olive oil
- 1 yellow onion, chopped
- 2 garlic cloves, minced
- 12 ounces risotto rice
- 4 cups chicken stock
- 1 big zucchini, grated
- ½ teaspoon nutmeg, ground
- 1 teaspoon thyme, chopped
- ½ teaspoon ginger, grated
- ½ teaspoon allspice, ground

Directions:
Set your instant pot on Sauté mode, add the oil, heat it up, add onion and garlic, stir and cook for 1-2 minutes.
Add the rest of the ingredients, toss, put the lid on and cook on High for 12 minutes.
Release the pressure fast for 5 minutes, divide the mix between plates and serve as a side dish.

Nutrition Value: calories 200, fat 7, fiber 4, carbs 7, protein 6

Spiced Carrot Rice

Preparation time: 5 minutes
Cooking time: 15 minutes
Serves: 4

Ingredients:
- 2 cups basmati rice
- 1 cup carrots, grated

- 2 cups chicken stock
- ½ teaspoon ginger, grated
- 3 garlic cloves, minced
- 2 tablespoons olive oil
- 1 yellow onion, chopped
- 1 tablespoon cumin, ground
- 1 teaspoon cloves, ground
- 1 teaspoon cardamom, ground
- 1 teaspoon sweet paprika
- A pinch of salt and black pepper

Directions:
Set the instant pot on sauté mode, add the oil, heat it up, add onion, carrots, garlic and ginger, stir and sauté for 3 minutes.
Add cumin, cloves, cardamom, paprika, salt and pepper, stir and cook for 2 minutes more.
Add the remaining ingredients, put the lid on and cook on High for 10 minutes.
Release the pressure fast for 5 minutes, stir the mix, divide between plates and serve as a side dish.

Nutrition Value: calories 200, fat 8, fiber 4, carbs 6, protein 8

Herbed Mash

Preparation time: 10 minutes
Cooking time: 10 minutes
Serves: 8

Ingredients:
- 2 garlic cloves, minced
- 3 pounds potatoes, peeled and cubed
- A pinch of salt and black pepper
- ¼ teaspoon sage, dried
- ½ teaspoon rosemary, dried
- ½ teaspoon thyme dried
- 1 and ½ cups water
- ¼ cup almond milk
- ½ cup parmesan, grated

Directions:
Add the water to the instant pot, add the steamer basket inside and put the potatoes in it.
Put the lid on and cook on High for 10 minutes.
Release the pressure naturally for 10 minutes, transfer the potatoes to a bowl and mash them with a potato masher.
Add the rest of the ingredients gradually, whisk well, divide between plates and serve as a side dish.

Nutrition Value: calories 181, fat 7, fiber 3, carbs 6, protein 7 Currant Rice

Preparation time: 10 minutes
Cooking time: 15 minutes
Serves: 6

Ingredients:
- 2 tablespoons olive oil
- ½ teaspoon chili powder
- ½ cup yellow onion, chopped
- 2 tablespoons coconut milk

- 1 and ½ cups Arborio rice
- 3 and ½ cups veggie stock
- A pinch of salt and black pepper
- ½ cup currants, chopped

Directions:
Set your instant pot on Sauté mode, add the oil, heat it up, add onion, stir and sauté for 5 minutes.
Add the rest of the ingredients, stir, put the lid on and cook on High for 10 minutes.
Release the pressure naturally for 10 minutes, divide between plates and serve as a side dish.

Nutrition Value: calories 184, fat 6, fiber 3, carbs 6, protein 6

Mint Farro Side Salad

Preparation time: 10 minutes
Cooking time: 30 minutes

Serves: 6

Ingredients:
- 1 tablespoon balsamic vinegar
- 1 cup whole grain farro
- 1 teaspoon lime juice
- A pinch of salt and black pepper
- 3 cups veggie stock
- 1 tablespoon olive oil
- ½ cup green onions, chopped
- 2 tablespoons mint leaves, chopped

Directions:
In your instant pot, combine the farro with salt, pepper and the stock, put the lid on and cook on High for 30 minutes.
Release the pressure naturally for 10 minutes, transfer the farro to a bowl, add the rest of the ingredients, toss, divide between plates and serve as a side dish.

Nutrition Value: calories 200, fat 8, fiber 3, carbs 7, protein 8

Lemon Spinach Rice

Preparation time: 10 minutes
Cooking time: 20 minutes

Serves: 4

Ingredients:
- 2 garlic cloves, minced
- 2 tablespoons olive oil
- ¾ cup yellow onion, chopped
- 1 and ½ cups white rice
- 12 ounces spinach, chopped
- 3 and ½ cups hot veggie stock
- A pinch of salt and black pepper
- 2 tablespoons lemon juice

Directions:

Set your instant pot on sauté mode, add the oil, heat it up, add garlic and onions, stir and sauté for 5 minutes.
Add the rest of the ingredients except the spinach, put the lid on and cook on High for 8 minutes.
Release the pressure fast for 5 minutes, add the spinach, toss, put the lid back on and cook on High for 3 minutes more.
Release the pressure fast again for 5 minutes, divide the mix between plates and serve as a side dish.

Nutrition Value: calories 200, fat 7, fiber 4, carbs 6, protein 5

Cheesy Thyme Rice

Preparation time: 10 minutes
Cooking time: 20 minutes

Serves: 4

Ingredients:
- 1 tablespoon olive oil
- 1 cup Arborio rice
- 2 garlic cloves, minced
- 2 cups chicken stock
- 16 ounces cream cheese
- 1 tablespoon parmesan, grated
- 1 and ½ tablespoons thyme, chopped
- A pinch of salt and black pepper

Directions:
Set your instant pot on Sauté mode, add the oil, heat up, add the garlic, stir and cook for 1 minute.
Add the rest of the ingredients, toss, put the lid on and cook on High for 20 minutes.
Release the pressure naturally for 10 minutes, divide the mix between plates and serve as a side dish.

Nutrition Value: calories 185, fat 6, fiber 4, carbs 6, protein 8

Greek Potato Mix

Preparation time: 10 minutes
Cooking time: 15 minutes

Serves: 6

Ingredients:
- ¼ cup chicken stock
- ½ cup yellow onion, chopped
- 2 tablespoons avocado oil
- 6 potatoes, peeled and cut into wedges
- A pinch of salt and black pepper
- ½ cup sour cream
- 1 tablespoon basil, chopped
- 1 cup mozzarella cheese, shredded

Directions:
Set your instant pot on Sauté mode, add the oil, heat it up, add the onion, stir and sauté for 3 minutes.
Add the potatoes, stock, salt and pepper, put the lid on and cook on High for 12 minutes.
Release the pressure naturally for 10 minutes, transfer the potato mix to a bowl, add the rest of the ingredients, toss and serve as side dish.

Nutrition Value: calories 200, fat 7, fiber 2, carbs 5, protein 6

Squash and Potato Mash

Preparation time: 10 minutes
Cooking time: 20 minutes

Serves: 4

Ingredients:
- ½ cup water
- 1 butternut squash, peeled and cubed
- 2 sweet potatoes, peeled and cubed
- A pinch of salt and black pepper
- 2 tablespoons butter
- ½ teaspoon nutmeg, grated

Directions:
1. Add the water to your instant pot, add steamer basket, add squash and sweet potatoes inside, put the lid on and cook on High for 20 minutes.
2. Release the pressure naturally for 10 minutes, transfer the mix to a bowl and mash well with a potato masher.
3. Add the rest of the ingredients, whisk well, divide between plates and serve as a side dish.

Nutrition Value: calories 126, fat 4, fiber 5, carbs 8, protein 5

Cinnamon Potatoes

Preparation time: 10 minutes
Cooking time: 25 minutes

Serves: 4

Ingredients:
- 3 pounds sweet potatoes, peeled and roughly cut into wedges
- 1 cup water
- ¼ cup coconut milk
- 1/3 cup coconut sugar
- ½ teaspoon nutmeg, ground
- 1 teaspoon cinnamon powder
- ¼ teaspoon allspice
- A pinch of cayenne pepper
- ¼ cup coconut, unsweetened and shredded

Directions:
Add the water to your instant pot, add steamer basket, add the potatoes into the basket, put the lid on and cook on High for 20 minutes.
Release the pressure fast for 5 minutes, drain the water, transfer the potatoes to a bowl and clean the instant pot.
In the clean instant pot, combine the potatoes with the rest of the ingredients except the coconut, put the lid on and cook on High for 5 minutes.
Release the pressure fast for 5 minutes, divide the mix between plates and serve as a side dish.

Nutrition Value: calories 175, fat 4, fiber 2, carbs 6, protein 8

Potato and Parsnip Wedges

Preparation time: 10 minutes
Cooking time: 12 minutes

Serves: 4

Ingredients:
- 4 potatoes, peeled and cut into wedges
- 2 parsnips, cut into wedges
- 1 cup water
- A pinch of salt and black pepper
- 1 tablespoon olive oil
- ¼ teaspoon sweet paprika
- ¼ teaspoon oregano, dried

Directions:
In a bowl, combine all the ingredients except the water and toss.
Put the water in the instant pot, add the steamer basket inside, put the vegetable wedges in the basket, put the lid on and cook on High for 12 minutes.
Release the pressure naturally for 10 minutes, divide the veggie wedges between plates and serve as a side dish.

Nutrition Value: calories 200, fat 5, fiber 3, carbs 6, protein 7

Balsamic Green Beans

Preparation time: 10 minutes
Cooking time: 12 minutes

Serves: 4

Ingredients:
- 1 pound fresh green beans, trimmed
- 2 spring onions, chopped
- 1 garlic clove, minced
- 2 cups tomatoes, cubed
- A pinch of salt and black pepper
- 1 tablespoon cilantro, chopped
- 1 tablespoon olive oil
- 2 teaspoons balsamic vinegar

Directions:
Set the pot on sauté mode, add the oil, heat it up, add the onions and garlic and sauté for 2 minutes.
Add the rest of the ingredients except the cilantro, toss, put the lid on and cook on High for 10 minutes.
Release the pressure naturally for 10 minutes, divide the mix between plates and serve as a side dish with the cilantro sprinkled on top.

Nutrition Value: calories 162, fat 6, fiber 2, carbs 6, protein 4

Quinoa Cucumber Salad

Preparation Time: 11 minutes

Serves: 4
Nutrition Values
- Calories:- 320
- Carbohydrate:- 31.2g
- Protein:- 12.1g
- Fat:- 18.5g
- Sugar:- 9.1g
- Sodium:- 0.27g

Ingredients
- 1/2 cucumber; chopped
- 1/2 cup quinoa; rinsed
- 3/4 cup water
- 1/4 tsp. salt
- 1/2 carrot; peeled and shredded
- 1/2 cup frozen edamame; thawed
- 3 green onions; chopped.
- 1 cup shredded red cabbage
- 1/2 tbsp. soy sauce
- 1 tbsp. lime juice
- 1 tbsp. vegetable oil
- 1 tbsp. freshly grated ginger
- 1 tbsp. sesame oil
- 2 tbsp. sugar
- pinch of red pepper flakes
- 1/2 cup peanuts; chopped.
- 1/4 cup freshly chopped cilantro
- 2 tbsp. chopped basil

Directions:
1. Add the quinoa, salt and water to Instant Pot.
2. Secure the lid and select the *Manual* function with high pressure for 1 minute,
3. When it beeps; do a quick release and remove the lid.
4. Meanwhile; add the remaining Ingredients to a bowl and mix well.
5. Add the cooked quinoa to the prepared mixture and mix well. Serve as a salad.

Lovely Lime Potatoes

Preparation Time: 15 minutes

Serves: 2
Nutrition Values
- Calories:- 225
- Carbohydrate:- 43.3g
- Protein:- 5.1g
- Fat:- 4.1g
- Sugar:- 3.2g
- Sodium:- 38mg

Ingredients
- 2 ½ medium potatoes; scrubbed and cubed
- 1/2 tbsp. olive oil
- 1 tbsp. fresh rosemary; chopped

- 1/2 cup vegetable broth
- 1 tbsp. fresh lemon juice
- Freshly ground black pepper to taste

Directions:
1. Put the oil, potatoes, pepper and rosemary to Instant Pot.
2. *Sauté* for 4 minutes with constant stirring.
3. Add all the remaining Ingredients into Instant Pot.
4. Secure the lid and select the *Manual* function for 6 minutes with high pressure,
5. Do a quick release after the beep then remove the lid. Give a gentle stir and serve warm.

Mashed Potatoes
Preparation Time: 23 minutes

Serves: 4
Nutrition Values
- Calories:- 394
- Carbohydrate:- 62.5g
- Protein:- 10.3g
- Fat:- 9.9g
- Sugar:- 8.5g
- Sodium:- 0.21g

Ingredients
- 6-8 medium potatoes (peeled
- 2 tbsp. full cream
- 2 cups water
- 1 tsp. coarse rock salt
- Additional salt and pepper to taste

Directions:
1. Add water, potatoes and salt to Instant Pot.
2. Secure the lid and select the *Manual* function for 18 minutes with high pressure,
3. When it beeps; do a Natural release in 10 minutes and remove the lid.
4. Drain the water from the pot and leave the potatoes inside,
5. Use a potato masher to mash the potatoes in the pot.
6. Stir in cream, pepper and additional salt. Mix well. Serve and enjoy.

Mac and Cheese
Preparation Time: 9 minutes

Serves: 4
Nutrition Values
- Calories:- 492
- Carbohydrate:- 33.9g
- Protein:- 25.4g
- Fat:- 28.3g
- Sugar:- 1.8g
- Sodium:- 0.49g

Ingredients
- 1/2 lb. pasta
- 1/2 cup Monterey Jack cheese
- 1/2 tbsp. dry mustard powder
- 1/2 tsp. hot sauce

- 1 tbsp. butter
- 2 cups water
- 1/2 cup of milk
- 1/2 lb. cheddar cheese

Directions:
1. Add water, pasta, hot sauce and dry mustard to Instant Pot
2. Secure the lid and select the *Manual* function for 4 minutes with high pressure,
3. Do a quick release after the beep then remove the lid.
4. Strain the pasta and return it back to the pot. Select the *Sauté* function to cook.
5. Add cheese, milk and butter to the pasta and let it melt. Stir and serve.

Easy Maple Glazed Brussel Sprouts

Preparation Time: 14 minutes

Serves: 4
Nutrition Values
- Calories:- 166
- Carbohydrate:- 14.5g
- Protein:- 3.9g
- Fat:- 11.4g
- Sugar:- 6.1g
- Sodium:- 0.14g

Ingredients
- 1 lb. Brussels sprouts (trimmed
- 1/2 tbsp. Earth Balance buttery spread
- 2 tbsp. freshly squeezed orange juice
- 1 tbsp. maple syrup
- 1/2 tsp. grated orange zest
- Black pepper; or to taste
- Salt; or to taste

Directions:
1. Add all the Ingredients to Instant Pot.
2. Secure the lid and select the *Manual* function for 4 minutes with high pressure,
3. Do a quick release after the beep, then remove the lid. Stir well and serve immediately.

Garlic with Beets

Preparation Time: 20 minutes

Serves: 4
Nutrition Values
- Calories:- 133
- Carbohydrate:- 17.4g
- Protein:- 2.3g
- Fat:- 7.3g
- Sugar:- 9g
- Sodium:- 1.32g

Ingredients
- 6 whole white beets
- 4 cups water
- 4 cloves garlic; minced
- 2 tbsp. olive oil

- 2 tbsp. lime juice
- 2 tsp. salt

Directions:
1. Separate the white part of the beets from the green ones, Wash and rinse,
2. Cut the white parts into cubes and add them to Instant Pot along with water.
3. Secure the lid and select the *Manual* function for 10 minutes with high pressure,
4. When it beeps; do a Natural release and remove the lid.
5. Now add the green parts of the beets to Instant Pot and let it stay for 5 minutes,
6. Strain the beets and set them aside,
7. Add oil and garlic to Instant Pot and *Sauté* for 2 minutes,
8. Return the beets to the pot and sauté for a minute, Drizzle lime juice and salt then serve.

Cabbage and Bacon

Preparation Time: 18 minutes

Serves: 4
Nutrition Values
- Calories:- 428
- Carbohydrate:- 30.7g
- Protein:- 34.4g
- Fat:- 24.7g
- Sugar:- 16.4g
- Sodium:- 1.48g

Ingredients
- 2 medium savoy cabbages; sliced into strips
- 6 oz. bacon; chopped.
- 2 tbsp. butter
- 2 small onions; sliced into strips
- 2 cups vegetable broth

Directions:
1. Add the butter, bacon and onions to Instant Pot and *Sauté* for 5 minutes,
2. Stir in cabbage and cook for another minute,
3. Pour the vegetable broth into the pot and secure the lid.
4. Select the *Manual* function with high pressure for 3 minutes,
5. When it beeps; do a Quick release and remove the lid. Serve and enjoy.

Dijon White Beans

Serves:3
Preparation Time: 30 minutes
Ingredients:

- 15 oz can cannellini beans, rinsed
- 1 tsp Dijon mustard
- 1 tbsp olive oil
- 1 tsp fresh thyme
- 1/4 small onion, sliced
- 1/2 bell pepper, chopped
- 1 tbsp vinegar
- Pepper
- Salt

Directions for Cooking:
1. Add bean into the instant pot and season with pepper and salt.
2. Seal pot with lid and cook on high for 20 minutes.
3. Allow to release pressure naturally for 10 minutes then release using quick release method.
4. Add remaining ingredients and stir well.
5. Serve and enjoy.

Nutrition Value:

Calories: 183; Carbohydrates: 25g; Protein: 9g; Fat: 4.8g; Sugar: 2.4g; Sodium: 180mg

Baked Potato

Serves:2
Preparation Time: 20 minutes
Ingredients:

- 2 large sweet potatoes
- 4 tbsp olive oil
- Pepper
- Salt

Directions for Cooking:
1. Pour 1 cup water into the instant pot and place steamer basket into the pot.
2. Cut sweet potatoes in half and season with pepper and salt.
3. Rub olive oil into the flesh of sweet potatoes.
4. Place sweet potato into the steamer basket.
5. Seal pot with lid and cook on high for 20 minutes.
6. Release pressure using quick release method than open the lid.
7. Serve and enjoy.

Nutrition Value:

Calories: 370; Carbohydrates: 33g; Protein: 2g; Fat: 28g; Sugar: 7g; Sodium: 123mg

Spiced Potatoes

Serves:4
Preparation Time: 10 minutes
Ingredients:

- 1 lb potatoes, cut into 1-inch cubes
- 2 tbsp Moroccan spice mix
- 2 tbsp coconut oil
- 1/2 lemon juice

Directions for Cooking:
1. Pour 1 cup water into the instant pot and place steamer basket into the pot.
2. Place potatoes into the steamer basket. Seal pot with lid and cook on for 5 minutes.
3. Release pressure using quick release method than open the lid.
4. Transfer potatoes on a plate and clean the instant pot.
5. Add oil into the pot and set the pot on sauté mode.
6. Return potatoes to the pot and sprinkle with the spice mix and cook until brown, about 5 minutes.
7. Transfer on serving dish and drizzle with lemon juice.
8. Serve and enjoy.

Nutrition Value:

Calories: 137; Carbohydrates: 17.8g; Protein: 1.9g; Fat: 6.9g; Sugar: 1.3g; Sodium: 7mg

Creamy Turnips Potato Mash

Serves: 4
Preparation Time: 9 minutes
Ingredients:

- 3 cups turnip, cubed
- 3 large potatoes, peeled and diced
- 1/4 cup chicken broth
- 2 tbsp coconut milk
- 1 cup water
- 3 tbsp butter
- 2 garlic cloves, chopped
- Pepper
- Salt

Directions for Cooking:
1. Pour 1 cup water into the instant pot and place steamer basket into the pot.
2. Place potatoes and turnip into the steamer basket.
3. Seal pot with lid and cook on high for 9 minutes.
4. Release pressure using quick release method than open the lid.
5. Transfer potato and turnip into the large bowl.
6. Clean the instant pot. Add butter and garlic to the pot and sauté until brown.
7. Transfer garlic butter mixture into the potato-turnip bowl and using masher mash until smooth.
8. Add broth, coconut milk, pepper, and salt and stir well.
9. Serve and enjoy.

Nutrition Value:

Calories: 317; Carbohydrates: 50.8g; Protein: 6.2g; Fat: 10.9g; Sugar: 7.2g; Sodium: 233mg

Potato Pumpkin Mash

Serves: 6
Preparation Time: 8 minutes
Ingredients:

- 8 potatoes, diced
- 1 tsp garlic powder
- 4 tbsp butter
- 1 1/2 cups vegetable stock
- 15 oz can pumpkin puree
- 2 tsp fresh thyme
- 1/4 tsp black pepper
- 1 tsp salt

Directions for Cooking:
1. Add broth and potatoes into the instant pot and stir well.
2. Seal pot with lid and cook on high for 8 minutes.
3. Release pressure using quick release method than open the lid.
4. Mash the potatoes using masher until smooth.
5. Add remaining ingredients into the pot and stir well.
6. Serve and enjoy.

Nutrition Value:

Calories: 374; Carbohydrates: 70.7g; Protein: 7.5g; Fat: 8.5g; Sugar: 13.9g; Sodium: 652mg

Dill Butter Potato

Serves: 4
Preparation Time: 15 minutes
Ingredients:

- 1 lb baby potatoes
- 2 tbsp butter
- 4 fresh dill sprigs
- 1 tbsp Celtic salt

Directions for Cooking:
1. Pour 1 cup water into the instant pot and place steamer basket into the pot.
2. Place baby potatoes into the steamer basket. Seal pot with lid and cook on high for 5 minutes.
3. Allow to release pressure naturally for 10 minutes then release using quick release method.
4. Transfer potatoes into the large bowl.
5. Add remaining ingredients and toss well.
6. Serve and enjoy.

Nutrition Value:

Calories: 117; Carbohydrates: 14.1g; Protein: 3g; Fat: 5.9g; Sugar: 0g; Sodium: 52mg

Chicken & Poultry

Chicken and Peppercorns

Preparation time: 5 minutes
Cooking time: 20 minutes

Serves: 4

Ingredients:
- 2 chicken breasts, skinless, boneless and cubed
- A pinch of salt and black pepper
- 1 teaspoon black peppercorns, crushed
- 4 garlic cloves, minced
- 1 cup chicken stock
- 1 tablespoon cilantro, chopped

Directions:
In your instant pot, mix the chicken with the rest of the ingredients except the cilantro, put the lid on and cook on High for 20 minutes.
Release the pressure fast for 5 minutes, divide everything between plates and serve with the cilantro sprinkled on top.

Nutrition Value: calories 221, fat 14, fiber 3, carbs 7, protein 14

Turkey and Tomato Sauce

Preparation time: 10 minutes
Cooking time: 25 minutes

Serves: 4

Ingredients:
- 1 turkey breast, skinless, boneless and cut into strips

- 2 tablespoons olive oil
- 1 yellow onion, chopped
- 4 ounces tomato sauce
- A handful cilantro, chopped
- A pinch of salt and black pepper
- ½ pound cherry tomatoes, halved
- 1 tablespoon parsley, chopped

Directions:
Set your instant pot on Sauté mode, add the oil, heat it up, add the onion and the meat and brown for 5 minutes.
Add the tomato sauce and the rest of the ingredients except the parsley, put the lid on and cook on High for 20 minutes.
Release the pressure naturally between plates, divide the turkey mix between plates, and serve with the parsley sprinkled on top.

Nutrition Value: calories 263, fat 14, fiber 1, carbs 8, protein 12

Ginger Turkey and Potatoes

Preparation time: 10 minutes
Cooking time: 25 minutes

Serves: 4

Ingredients:
- 1 turkey breast, skinless, boneless and sliced
- A pinch of salt and black pepper
- 1 tablespoon avocado oil
- 1 tablespoon ginger, grated
- 1 tablespoon sweet paprika
- 2 gold potatoes, peeled and cubed
- 2 garlic cloves, minced
- 1 and ½ cups chicken stock
- 2 green onions, chopped
- 1 tablespoon cilantro, chopped

Directions:
Set your instant pot on Sauté mode, add the oil, heat it up, add the ginger, paprika, garlic and the meat and brown for 5 minutes.
Add the rest of the ingredients, put the lid on and cook on High for 20 minutes.
Release the pressure naturally for 10 minutes, divide everything between plates and serve.

Nutrition Value: calories 263, fat 12, fiber 3, carbs 6, protein 14

Turkey and Carrots Mix

Preparation time: 10 minutes
Cooking time: 20 minutes

Serves: 4

Ingredients:
- 1 big turkey breast, skinless, boneless and sliced
- 1 tablespoon olive oil

- 1 pound baby carrots
- 1 teaspoon chili powder
- 1 teaspoon oregano, dried
- 1 and ½ cups chicken stock
- 2 tablespoons tomato sauce
- A pinch of salt and black pepper

Directions:
Set the instant pot on Sauté mode, add the oil, heat it up, add the meat and brown for 5 minutes.
Add the carrots and the rest of the ingredients, put the lid on and cook on High for 15 minutes.
Release the pressure naturally for 10 minutes, divide the mix between plates and serve.

Nutrition Value: calories 253, fat 13, fiber 2, carbs 7, protein 16

Creamy Turkey

Preparation time: 10 minutes
Cooking time: 20 minutes

Serves: 4

Ingredients:
- 1 big turkey breast, skinless, boneless and cubed
- 1 yellow onion, chopped
- 4 garlic cloves, minced
- ¼ cup parsley, chopped
- A pinch of salt and black pepper
- 1 teaspoon oregano, dried
- 1 cup coconut milk
- 1 cup chicken stock
- 2 tablespoons olive oil

Directions:
Set your instant pot on Sauté mode, add the oil, heat it up, add the onion, garlic and the turkey and brown for 5 minutes.
Add the rest of the ingredients, toss, put the lid on and cook on High for 15 minutes.
Release the pressure naturally for 10 minutes, divide everything between plates and serve.

Nutrition Value: calories 234, fat 14, fiber 4, carbs 7, protein 15

Sage Turkey and Sweet Potatoes

Preparation time: 5 minutes
Cooking time: 30 minutes

Serves: 4

Ingredients:
- 1 turkey breast, skinless, boneless and sliced
- 1 yellow onion, chopped
- 3 garlic cloves, minced
- 1 cup chicken stock
- A pinch of salt and black pepper
- 2 tablespoons olive oil
- 1 tablespoon sage, chopped

- 2 sweet potatoes, cubed
- 1 tablespoon chives, chopped

Directions:
Set pot on Sauté mode, add the oil, heat it up, add the onion, garlic and the turkey and brown for 5 minutes.
Add the stock and the rest of the ingredients, put the lid on and cook on High for 25 minutes.
Release the pressure fast for 5 minutes, divide the turkey and the sweet potatoes between plates and serve.

Nutrition Value: calories 263, fat 13, fiber 2, carbs 7, protein 15

Chicken and Ginger Asparagus

Preparation time: 10 minutes
Cooking time: 20 minutes

Serves: 4

Ingredients:
- 4 chicken breasts, skinless, boneless and halved
- 1 asparagus bunch, trimmed and steamed
- 1 cup tomato sauce
- 1 cup chicken stock
- ½ teaspoon chili powder
- 1 teaspoon basil, chopped
- 1 teaspoon oregano, chopped
- A pinch of salt and black pepper

Directions:
In your instant pot, mix the chicken with the tomato sauce and the rest of the ingredients except the asparagus, put the lid on and cook on High for 15 minutes.
Release the pressure naturally for 10 minutes, set the pot on Sauté mode again, add the asparagus, cook for 5 minutes more, divide everything between plates and serve.

Nutrition Value: calories 200, fat 13, fiber 2, carbs 5, protein 16

Balsamic Chicken

Preparation time: 5 minutes
Cooking time: 20 minutes

Serves: 4

Ingredients:
- 2 chicken breasts, skinless, boneless and halved
- 1 and ½ cups chicken stock
- A pinch of salt and black pepper
- 1 tablespoon mustard
- 3 garlic cloves, minced
- 1 tablespoon balsamic vinegar
- 1 tablespoon avocado oil

Directions:
Set the instant pot on Sauté mode, add the oil, heat it up, add the garlic and the chicken and brown for 2 minutes.
Add the stock and the rest of the ingredients, put the lid on and cook on High for 18 minutes.

Release the pressure fast for 5 minutes, divide the mix between plates and serve.

Nutrition Value: calories 200, fat 12, fiber 2, carbs 6, protein 15

Turkey and Ginger Rice

Preparation time: 5 minutes
Cooking time: 25 minutes

Serves: 4

Ingredients:
- 1 big turkey breast, skinless, boneless and sliced
- 1 shallot, sliced
- 1 tablespoon olive oil
- 3 garlic cloves, minced
- A pinch of salt and black pepper
- 2 cups chicken stock
- 1 cup wild rice
- 1 tablespoon ginger, grated
- 1 green bell pepper, chopped
- 1 cup coconut milk
- 1 and ½ teaspoon turmeric powder
- 1 tablespoon cilantro, chopped

Directions:
Set the instant pot on Sauté mode, add the oil, heat it up, add the shallots and the garlic and sauté for 2 minutes.
Add the meat and brown for 2 minutes more.
Add the stock, rice and the rest of the ingredients, put the lid on and cook on High for 20 minutes.
Release the pressure fast for 5 minutes, divide the mix between plates and serve.

Nutrition Value: calories 253, fat 14, fiber 2, carbs 7, protein 16

Rosemary Chicken and Green Beans

Preparation time: 10 minutes
Cooking time: 20 minutes

Serves: 4

Ingredients:
- 4 garlic cloves, chopped
- 2 chicken breasts, skinless and halved
- 1 yellow onion, sliced
- 1 teaspoon rosemary, dried
- 1 cup chicken stock
- A pinch of salt and black pepper
- 1 cup tomato puree
- 1 cup green beans, trimmed and halved

Directions:
In your instant pot, mix the chicken with the rest of the ingredients, put the lid on and cook on High for 20 minutes.
Release the pressure naturally for 10 minutes, divide the mix between plates and serve.

Nutrition Value: calories 273, fat 13, fiber 3, carbs 7, protein 17

Scampi Chicken

Preparation Time: 20 minutes

Serves: 6
Nutrition Values
- Calories:- 480
- Carbohydrate:- 12.5g
- Protein:- 68g
- Fat:- 14.3g
- Sugar:- 1.9g
- Sodium:- 0.33g

Ingredients
- 3 chicken breasts; cut into strips
- ½ red onion sliced
- 1 red bell pepper sliced
- 3 cloves of garlic minced
- 1 cup white wine
- 1/2 cup parmesan cheese
- 1/2 tsp. pepper
- 1/2 cup chicken broth
- 1/2 tsp. garlic powder
- 1/2 tsp. Italian seasoning
- 1 yellow bell pepper sliced
- 2 tbsp. olive oil
- ½ cup flour
- 1 tsp. salt

Directions:
1. Select the *Sauté* function on your instant pot pressure cooker. Allow it to preheat for 5 minutes,
2. Meanwhile put the flour, salt and pepper into a shallow container. Add the chicken strips to the dry mix and dredge it through to get an even coating.
3. Now put the oil into the preheated cooker and place chicken in it.
4. Let it cook for 3 minutes; from each side, until it turns golden brown.
5. Add the peppers, garlic cloves, onions, chicken broth and wine,
6. Cover with the cooker lid. Using the *Manual* function, set the timer for 5 minutes and cook at high pressure,
7. When it beeps; do a *Quick Release* then open the lid.
8. Add parmesan cheese to the pot immediately. Stir it well in. Serve over pasta.

Turkey Breasts with Basil and Tomato Sauce

Preparation Time: 35 minutes

Serves: 4
Nutrition Values
- Calories:- 355
- Carbohydrate:- 11.5g
- Protein:- 36.5g
- Fat:- 18.3g
- Sugar:- 5.6g
- Sodium:- 0.62g

Ingredients
- 1 pound turkey breast cut into long strips
- 15 oz. fire roasted tomatoes
- 3 tbsp. olive oil
- Salt and pepper to taste
- 5 cloves garlic; minced
- 8 leaves basil; chopped.
- 1/2 cup heavy cream; 125 mL

Directions:
1. Put the roasted tomatoes in a blender and blend to form a smooth puree, Put it to one side,
2. Sprinkle salt and pepper over the chicken breasts for seasoning.
3. Add olive oil to the instant pot and select the *Sauté* function. Add the turkey breasts to the pot and cook until golden brown.
4. Now remove the turkey breasts and put them aside,
5. Add the oil, garlic and basil to the pot and *Sauté* for 1 minute,
6. Pour the tomato paste and heavy cream into the pot and let it cook for 2-3 minutes,
7. Now put the turkey breasts into the sauce and secure the lid.
8. Select *Manual* function to high pressure for 15 minutes,
9. When it beeps; release the steam and remove the lid. Garnish with basil leaves,

Special Chicken Masala

Preparation Time: 30 minutes

Serves: 4
Nutrition Values
- Calories:- 1315
- Carbohydrate:- 30.9g
- Protein:- 78.6g
- Fat:- 0.8g
- Sugar:- 2.7g
- Sodium:- 0.87g

Ingredients
- 2 boneless/skinless chicken breasts; cut in half
- 3 tbsp. olive oil
- 1/2 cup potato starch
- 1/2 tsp. black pepper
- 1/2 cup chicken broth
- 3 oz. Prosciutto; diced
- ½ tsp. Herbs de Provence
- 2 large shallots
- 3 sprigs fresh thyme
- 2 tbsp. butter
- 3 cloves fresh garlic; minced
- 1 pound Cremini mushrooms; sliced
- 1 cup dry Marsala wine
- 1 tbsp. kosher salt
- Parsley for garnish

Directions:
1. In a shallow bowl; mix the potato starch, pepper and salt. Add the chicken slices to the mix.
2. Coat the chicken evenly with the starch mix.
3. Select the *Sauté* function on your instant pot. Add the oil and chicken to the pot.
4. Cook the chicken cutlets on each side until they turn golden brown.

5. Remove the chicken from the pot. Add the Prosciutto, 1/4 cup of marsala wine mushrooms and the shallots to the pot.
6. Sauté the Ingredients for 3 minutes, Then add the garlic.
7. Stir in remaining the Marsala wine to and cook until it bubbles,
8. Add the chicken stock thyme and the Herb de Provence then secure the lid.
9. Cook at high pressure for 2 minutes using the *Manual* function.
10. Switch off the cooker and release the steam naturally. Garnish the chicken with parsley and serve.

Turkey and Smoked Paprika

Preparation Time: 60 minutes

Serves: 6
Nutrition Values
- Calories:- 903
- Carbohydrate:- 5.4g
- Protein:- 96.4g
- Fat:- 13.2g
- Sugar:- 0.4g
- Sodium:- 0.49g

Ingredients
- 1 pound turkey thighs
- 2 tbsp. smoked paprika
- 1/2 tsp. red pepper flakes
- 1/2 cup olive oil
- 8 cloves garlic minced
- 1/4 cup parsley fresh; chopped.
- 2 tbsp. oregano fresh; chopped.
- 1/2 tsp. black pepper.
- 1/2 cup water
- 1/2 tsp. salt.

Directions:

1. Pour the oil into the instant pot. Select the *Sauté* function.
2. Add the garlic; smoked paprika, herbs and red pepper flakes, Cook for 1 minute,
3. Add salt and pepper to taste,
4. Pour this mixture over the turkey thighs, generously coating them.
5. Add the water to the pot. Place a trivet inside,
6. Put the coated turkey thighs on the trivet.
7. Secure the lid. Set the *Manual* function to high pressure for 50 minutes,
8. When it beeps; release the steam naturally then remove the lid.
9. Take out the turkey thighs and slice them. Sprinkle fresh parsley and oregano to serve.

Chicken with Lime Juice

Preparation Time: 35 minutes

Serves: 6
Nutrition Values
- Calories:- 748
- Carbohydrate:4.3g
- Protein:- 127.5g
- Fat:- 19.9g
- Sugar:- 4.4g
- Sodium:- 0.65g

Ingredients
- 2 pounds' chicken thighs; boneless,
- 2 tbsp. olive oil
- 1/4 cup lemon juice
- 3/4 cup chicken broth
- 2 tbsp. Italian seasoning
- 3 pounds red potatoes; quartered
- 3 tbsp. Dijon mustard
- Salt and pepper

Directions:
1. Place the oil and the chicken in the instant pot. Sprinkle salt and pepper to taste,
2. In a separate bowl; combine the lemon juice chicken broth and the Dijon mustard and mix them well.
3. Now add the potatoes, cut into 4 pieces, along with the remaining seasoning.
4. Secure the lid and select the *Manual* option - 15 minutes at high pressure,
5. Let it cook until the beep. Release the steam over 15 minutes using the *Natural Release* method. Serve.

Amazing Turkey Stuffed Tacos

Preparation Time: 25 minutes

Serves: 6
Nutrition Values
- Calories:- 675
- Carbohydrate:8.2g
- Protein:- 78.7g
- Fat:- 19.1g
- Sugar:- 3.7g
- Sodium:0.89g

Ingredients
- ¾ lb. chopped white turkey meat
- 2 tbsp. olive oil
- 1 medium onion
- 3 cloves garlic
- 1 jalapeno pepper; diced
- 1 tsp. cumin
- 1/2 bottle of any dark beer
- 4 diced tomatoes
- 8 taco shells
- Salt and pepper to taste

Toppings:
- Tomatoes
- Lettuce
- Salsa
- Cheddar cheese

Directions:
1. Put the olive oil, chopped onion and garlic into the instant pot.
2. Select the *Sauté* function and let it cook for 5 minutes,
3. Add the jalapeno pepper and chopped turkey to the pot.
4. Let it cook for 5 minutes,
5. Now add the salt, pepper, cumin and diced tomatoes,
6. After 5 minutes more cooking, pour in the beer.

7. Now cover the lid and lock it properly. Select the *Manual* function - 5 minutes at high pressure,
8. When it beeps; use the *Natural Release* to release all the steam.
9. Remove the cooker lid but leave the prepared filling to one side, To serve; stuff the filling in a taco wrap and add cheese on top.

Juicy Chicken Tacos

Preparation Time: 35 minutes

Serves: 12
Nutrition Values
- Calories:- 110
- Carbohydrate:- 13.3g
- Protein:- 10.8g
- Fat:- 1.7g
- Sugar:- 0.7g
- Sodium:- 0.42g

Ingredients
- 4 skinless; boneless chicken breasts

For Mojo:
- 1/4 cup olive oil
- ⅔ cup fresh lime juice
- 8 garlic cloves; minced
- 1 tbsp. dried oregano
- 1 tbsp. grated orange peel
- 1/4 tsp. ground black pepper
- ⅔ cup orange juice
- 2 tsp. ground cumin
- 2 tsp. kosher salt
- 1/2 cup chopped fresh cilantro

For Serving:
- 12 organic corn tortillas
- 1/2 cup red onion; finely diced
- Chopped cilantro.
- 1 avocado; sliced

Directions:
1. Put all the Ingredients of mojo into a small bowl and mix together.
2. Put the chicken in the pot and pour the mojo mix over it.
3. Cover with the cooker lid and select the *poultry* function with 20 minutes on the timer.
4. When it beeps; use *Natural Release* for 10 minutes then *Quick Release* to remove all the steam.
5. Remove the lid carefully. Shred the chicken inside the pot using two forks,
6. To make the chicken crispier, broil it in an oven for 8 minutes, Serve it with tacos, onion, avocado and fresh cilantro on top.

Beef, lamb & pork

Beef and Artichokes

Preparation time: 10 minutes
Cooking time: 45 minutes

Serves: 6

Ingredients:
- 2 pounds beef roast, cubed
- 1 tablespoon olive oil
- A pinch of salt and black pepper
- 2 cups beef stock
- 12 ounces canned artichokes, drained
- 1 tablespoon capers, drained and chopped
- 2 tomatoes, cubed
- 1 tablespoon parsley, chopped
- ½ teaspoon smoked paprika
- 1 yellow onion, chopped
- 4 garlic cloves, minced

Directions:
Set the instant pot on Sauté mode, add the oil, heat it up, add the onion and the garlic and sauté for 5 minutes.
Add the meat and brown for 5 minutes more.
Add the rest of the ingredients, put the lid on and cook on High for 35 minutes.
Release the pressure naturally for 10 minutes, divide the mix between plates and serve.

Nutrition Value: calories 264, fat 14, fiber 4, carbs 6, protein 17

Lemony Beef Mix

Preparation time: 10 minutes
Cooking time: 35 minutes

Serves: 4

Ingredients:
- 2 tablespoons avocado oil
- 1 and ½ pounds beef stew meat, cubed
- 1 red onion, chopped
- 2 tablespoons lemon juice
- 2 garlic cloves, minced
- 2 cups beef stock
- A pinch of salt and black pepper
- ½ teaspoon thyme, dried
- ½ bunch basil, chopped

Directions:
Set the instant pot on Sauté mode, add the oil, heat it up, add the meat, onion and garlic and cook for 5 minutes.
Add the rest of the ingredients, put the lid on and cook on High for 30 minutes.
Release the pressure naturally for 10 minutes, divide the mix between plates and serve.

Nutrition Value: calories 263, fat 14, fiber 3, carbs 7, protein 20

Beef and Shallots Sauce

Preparation time: 10 minutes
Cooking time: 35 minutes

Serves: 4

Ingredients:
- 6 shallots, chopped
- 2 pounds beef stew meat, cubed
- 2 cups beef stock
- 2 garlic cloves, minced
- 2 tablespoons chives, chopped
- 1 teaspoon sage, dried
- ½ teaspoon oregano, dried
- A pinch of salt and black pepper
- 2 tablespoons olive oil

Directions:
Set your instant pot on Sauté mode, add the oil, heat it up, add the garlic and the shallots and sauté for 5 minutes.
Add the meat and brown for 5 minutes more.
Add the rest of the ingredients, put the lid on and cook on High for 25 minutes.
Release the pressure naturally for 10 minutes, divide the beef and shallots sauce between plates and serve.

Nutrition Value: calories 263, fat 14, fiber 5, carbs 7, protein 15

Cheesy Beef and Carrots

Preparation time: 10 minutes
Cooking time: 30 minutes

Serves: 4

Ingredients:
- 1 and ½ pound beef stew meat, cubed
- 12 ounces mozzarella cheese, shredded
- 1 tablespoon olive oil
- 1 red onion, chopped
- 2 spring onions, chopped
- 4 carrots, sliced
- 1 and ½ cups beef stock
- 1 tablespoon parsley, chopped
- A pinch of salt and black pepper

Directions:
Set your instant pot on Sauté mode, add the oil, heat it up, add the red and spring onion and cook for 2 minutes.
Add the meat and brown it for 5 minutes.
Add the rest of the ingredients except the parsley and the cheese, put the lid on and cook on High for 22 minutes.
Release the pressure naturally for 10 minutes, sprinkle the cheese all over the beef mix, leave aside for a few minutes, divide everything between plates and serve.

Nutrition Value: calories 253, fat 14, fiber 3, carbs 7, protein 17

Beef and Zucchini Mix

Preparation time: 10 minutes
Cooking time: 30 minutes

Serves: 4

Ingredients:
- 2 tablespoons chili paste
- 1 cup beef stock
- 1 tablespoon olive oil
- 2 pounds beef steak, cubed
- ¼ teaspoon red pepper flakes
- A pinch of salt and black pepper
- 3 zucchinis, cubed
- 2 spring onions, chopped

Directions:
Set your instant pot on Sauté mode, add the oil, heat it up, add the meat and brown for 5 minutes.
Add the chili paste and the rest of the ingredients except the zucchinis and the spring onion, put the lid on and cook on High for 20 minutes.
Release the pressure fast for 5 minutes, add the zucchinis, put the lid back on and cook on High for 5 minutes more.
Release the pressure fast for 5 minutes more, divide the mix between plates, sprinkle the spring onion on top and serve.

Nutrition Value: calories 276, fat 14, fiber 3, carbs 7, protein 20

Cinnamon Beef and Asparagus

Preparation time: 10 minutes
Cooking time: 30 minutes

Serves: 4

Ingredients:
- 2 pounds chuck roast, cubed
- 1 tablespoon avocado oil
- 1 yellow onion, chopped
- 1 cup beef stock
- 1 pound asparagus, trimmed and halved
- 2 teaspoons sweet paprika
- 1 and ½ teaspoons cinnamon powder
- 1 tablespoon chives, chopped

Directions:
Set your instant pot on Sauté mode, add the oil, heat it up, add the onion and sauté for 2 minutes.
Add the meat and brown for 3 minutes more.
Add the rest of the ingredients except the asparagus and the chives, toss, put the lid on and cook on High for 20 minutes.
Release the pressure naturally for 10 minutes, set the pot on Sauté mode again, add the asparagus and the chives, toss gently and cook for 5 minutes more.
Divide the mix between plates and serve.

Nutrition Value: calories 287, fat 16, fiber 4, carbs 6, protein 20

Beef and Red Cabbage Mix

Preparation time: 10 minutes
Cooking time: 40 minutes

Serves: 4

Ingredients:
- 2 and ½ pounds beef roast, cubed
- 2 cups beef stock
- 3 garlic cloves, chopped
- 1 red cabbage head, shredded
- A pinch of salt and black pepper
- 1 cup tomato puree
- 1 tablespoon cilantro, chopped

Directions:
In your instant pot, combine the beef with the rest of the ingredients except the cabbage and the cilantro, toss, put the lid on and cook on High for 30 minutes.
Release the pressure fast for 5 minutes, add the cabbage, put the lid back on and cook on High for 10 minutes more.
Release the pressure fast for 5 more minutes, divide the beef and cabbage mix between plates, sprinkle the cilantro on top and serve.

Nutrition Value: calories 264, fat 8, fiber 3, carbs 6, protein 17

Cheesy Lamb

Preparation time: 10 minutes
Cooking time: 30 minutes

Serves: 4

Ingredients:
- 1 and ½ pound lamb shanks
- 2 tablespoons olive oil
- 1 yellow onion, chopped
- 2 garlic cloves, minced
- 2 tablespoons tomato sauce
- 1 teaspoon rosemary, dried
- 2 cups beef stock
- A pinch of salt and black pepper
- ¼ cup goat cheese, crumbled
- 1 tablespoon cilantro, chopped

Directions:
Set your instant pot on Sauté mode, add the oil, heat it up, add the meat and brown for 3 minutes.
Add the onion, garlic and rosemary and cook for 2 minutes more.
Add the rest of the ingredients except the cheese and cilantro, put the lid on and cook on High for 25 minutes.
Release the pressure naturally for 10 minutes, add the cheese and the cilantro, leave the mix aside for a few minutes, divide everything between plates and serve.

Nutrition Value: calories 275, fat 13, fiber 4, carbs 7, protein 20

Sage Lamb Ribs

Preparation time: 10 minutes
Cooking time: 25 minutes

Serves: 4

Ingredients:
- 4 lamb ribs
- 4 garlic cloves, minced
- 1 tablespoon sage, chopped
- 1 and ½ cups veggie stock
- 2 tablespoons olive oil
- A pinch of salt and black pepper
- 2 tomatoes, cubed

Directions:
Set your instant pot on Sauté mode, add the oil, heat it up, add the lamb, garlic, sage, salt and pepper and brown for 5 minutes.
Add the stock and the tomatoes, put the lid on and cook on High for 20 minutes.
Release the pressure naturally for 10 minutes, divide the lamb between plates and serve.

Nutrition Value: calories 263, fat 12, fiber 4, carbs 7, protein 12

Herbed Lamb Shanks

Preparation time: 10 minutes
Cooking time: 40 minutes

Serves: 4

Ingredients:
- 4 lamb shanks
- 2 tablespoons olive oil
- A pinch of salt and black pepper
- 1 teaspoon marjoram, dried
- 1 teaspoon rosemary, dried
- 1 teaspoon sage, dried
- 1 teaspoon thyme, dried
- 3 garlic cloves, minced
- 2 cups veggie stock

Directions:
Set your instant pot on Sauté mode, add the oil, heat it up, add the meat and brown for 4 minutes.
Add the rest of the ingredients, put the lid on and cook on High for 35 minutes.
Release the pressure naturally for 10 minutes, divide the lamb between plates and serve with a side salad.

Nutrition Value: calories 263, fat 12, fiber 3, carbs 7, protein 10

Pork Chops and Apples

Preparation time: 5 minutes
Cooking time: 25 minutes

Serves: 4

Ingredients:
- 4 pork chops

- 2 tablespoons avocado oil
- 1 garlic clove, minced
- 2 tablespoons lemon juice
- 2 green apples, cored and cubed
- 1 yellow onion, chopped
- ½ cup beef stock
- A pinch of salt and black pepper
- 1 tablespoon parsley, chopped

Directions:
Set your instant pot on Sauté mode, add the oil, heat it up, add the onion and garlic and sauté for 2 minutes.
Add the pork chops and cook for 3 minutes.
Add the rest of the ingredients except the parsley, put the lid on and cook on High for 20 minutes.
Release the pressure fast for 5 minutes, divide everything between plates and serve.

Nutrition Value: calories 210, fat 5, fiber 3, carbs 8, protein 12

Pork and Parsley Sauce

Preparation time: 10 minutes
Cooking time: 20 minutes

Serves: 4

Ingredients:
- 4 pork chops
- 2 tablespoons olive oil
- 2 teaspoons chili powder
- 1 cup coconut cream
- 2 garlic cloves, minced
- Salt and black pepper to the taste
- 1 small bunch parsley, chopped

Directions:
In a blender, combine the parsley with the oil, cream, garlic, chili powder, salt and pepper and pulse well.
Put the pork chops in your instant pot, add the parsley sauce, toss, put the lid on and cook on High for 20 minutes.
Release the pressure naturally for 10 minutes, divide the mix between plates and serve.

Nutrition Value: calories 248, fat 11, fiber 3, carbs 6, protein 15

Tomato Pork Chops

Preparation time: 10 minutes
Cooking time: 25 minutes

Serves: 4

Ingredients:
- 4 pork chops
- 1 cup veggie stock
- ¼ cup tomato puree
- 4 teaspoons sweet paprika
- A pinch of salt and black pepper

Directions:
In your instant pot, combine the pork chops with the rest of the ingredients, put the lid on and cook on High for 25 minutes.
Release the pressure naturally for 10 minutes, divide everything between plates and serve.

Nutrition Value: calories 233, fat 9, fiber 3, carbs 7, protein 14

Pork and Endives

Preparation time: 10 minutes
Cooking time: 25 minutes

Serves: 4

Ingredients:
- 4 pork chops
- 2 tablespoons olive oil
- A pinch of salt and black pepper
- 2 garlic cloves, minced
- 1 yellow onion, chopped
- 1 cup chicken stock
- 2 endives, sliced
- ¼ cup tomato sauce
- 1 tablespoon parsley, chopped

Directions:
Set your instant pot on Sauté mode, add the oil, heat it up, add the onion and garlic and sauté for 2 minutes.
Add the meat and cook for 3 minutes more.
Add the rest of the ingredients, put the lid on and cook on High for 20 minutes.
Release the pressure naturally for 10 minutes, divide the mix between plates and serve.

Nutrition Value: calories 227, fat 14, fiber 4, carbs 6, protein 16

Sesame Pork Chops

Preparation time: 10 minutes
Cooking time: 25 minutes

Serves: 4

Ingredients:
- 4 pork chops
- 2 teaspoons sesame seeds
- 1 tablespoon olive oil
- 1 teaspoon chili powder
- 1 teaspoon sweet paprika
- 1 cup tomato sauce
- 1 tablespoon chives, chopped

Directions:
Set your instant pot on Sauté mode, add the oil, heat it up, add the pork chops and brown for 5 minutes.
Add the rest of the ingredients except the sesame seeds, put the lid on and cook on High for 20 minutes.
Release the pressure naturally for 10 minutes, divide the pork chops between plates, sprinkle the sesame seeds on top and serve.

Nutrition Value: calories 236, fat 12, fiber 2, carbs 7, protein 15

Pork and Fennel

Preparation time: 10 minutes
Cooking time: 25 minutes

Serves: 4

Ingredients:
- 1 and ½ pounds pork loin, cubed
- 1 cup stock
- 2 fennel bulbs, sliced
- 2 tablespoons lemon juice
- 2 tablespoons olive oil
- ¼ cup garlic powder
- 1 tablespoon sweet paprika
- A pinch of salt and black pepper

Directions:
Set the instant pot on Sauté mode, add the oil, heat it up, add the meat and brown for 5 minutes. Add the rest of the ingredients, put the lid on and cook on High for 20 minutes. Release the pressure naturally for 10 minutes, divide the mix between plates and serve.

Nutrition Value: 273, fat 12, fiber 4, carbs 7, protein 17

Mexican Butter Beef Recipe

Preparation Time: 55 minutes

Serves: 3
Nutrition Values
- Calories:- 649
- Carbohydrate:4.1g
- Protein:- 23.9g
- Fat:- 59g
- Sugar:- 1.2g
- Sodium:- 0.75g

Ingredients
- 1 pound boneless beef
- 1/2 tsp. black pepper
- 1/2 medium onion; thinly sliced
- 1 tbsp. butter
- 1/2 tbsp. tomato paste
- 1/4 tsp. red boat fish sauce
- 3 garlic cloves; minced
- 1/4 cup bone broth
- 1/2 tbsp. chili powder
- 3/4 tsp. salt

Directions:
1. Add the chili powder and salt to the beef in a bowl. Mix well.
2. Heat the butter in the instant pot on the *Sauté* function.
3. Sauté the onion for 4 minutes then add the tomato paste and garlic.
4. Add the fish sauce, beef and broth to the cooker and lock the lid.

5. Select the *meat stew* function and cook for 30 minutes at high pressure,
6. Natural release the steam for 15 minutes then remove the lid. Sprinkle some salt and pepper on top then serve.

Mushroom Beef Stroganoff

Preparation Time: 40 minutes

Serves: 6
Nutrition Values
- Calories:- 317
- Carbohydrate:- 4.4g
- Protein:- 36.4g
- Fat:- 16.6g
- Sugar:- 1.1g
- Sodium:- 0.67g

Ingredients
- 1 ½ lbs. beef stew meat
- 1 ½ tbsp. oil
- 1 ½ tbsp. garlic
- 1 ½ tsp. black pepper
- 3/4 cup sour cream
- 3/4 cup diced onions
- 1 ½ tsp. salt
- 2 cups mushroom; chopped.
- 1 cup water

Directions:

1. Select the *Sauté* function on the instant pot.
2. Add the oil. the onions and garlic. Cook for 3 minutes,
3. Add the remaining ingredients, except the sour cream.
4. Secure the lid and set the cooker on *Manual* for 20 minutes at high pressure,
5. When it beeps; *Natural Release* the steam and remove the lid after 20 minutes, Stir in the sour cream and serve.

Lamb Curry Recipe

Preparation Time: 65 minutes

Serves: 4
Nutrition Values
- Calories:- 340
- Carbohydrate:7.1g
- Protein:- 29.5g
- Fat:- 21.3g
- Sugar:- 4.3g
- Sodium:- 0.17g

Ingredients
- 1 pound grass-fed lamb shoulder; cut into bite-sized pieces
- 1 tbsp. curry powder; divided
- 1/4 cup unsweetened coconut milk
- 1 tbsp. fresh lemon juice
- 2 tbsp. fresh basil; chopped
- 2 tbsp. coconut cream
- 1 tbsp. coconut oil
- 1 medium yellow onion; chopped.

- 1/2 cup chicken broth
- Salt and black pepper to taste

Directions:
1. Combine the coconut cream, milk and curry powder in a bowl and then add the lamb. Allow to marinate for 20 minutes,
2. Heat the oil and butter in the instant pot on *Sauté* function.
3. Stir in the onion and garlic and cook for 4 minutes,
4. Add the curry powder to the pot and cook for a minute,
5. Now put the lamb into the pot, keeping the marinade to one side,
6. Stir in the chicken broth pepper, salt and lemon juice then secure the lid.
7. Cook on *Manual* setting at high pressure for 20 minutes,
8. *Quick Release* the steam, remove the lid and add the cream marinade to the lamb.
9. Cook for 5 minutes on *Sauté* mode, Serve with fresh basil on top.

Beef and Bacon Casserole

Preparation Time: 50 minutes

Serves: 4
Nutrition Values
- Calories:- 823
- Carbohydrate:6.7g
- Protein:- 72.9g
- Fat:- 54.9g
- Sugar:- 3.2g
- Sodium:- 1.88g

Ingredients
- 1/2 pound bacon; cooked and chopped.
- 1-pound ground beef
- 1/4 tsp. onion powder
- 4 eggs
- 1/2 cup heavy cream
- 1/4 tsp. ground pepper
- 6 oz. cheddar cheese; grated
- 1 ½ garlic cloves
- 3 oz. tomato paste
- 1/4 tsp. salt

Directions:
1. Put the beef, bacon, garlic and onion powder into the instant pot and *Sauté* for 5 minutes,
2. Combine the cream, eggs, salt, tomato paste and cheddar cheese, in a bowl.
3. Pour this mixture over the beef and bacon. Secure the lid.
4. Cook on the *Manual* function for 25 minutes at high pressure,
5. *Natural release* the steam for 5 minutes then remove the lid. Serve hot.

Special Lamb Stew

Preparation Time: 60 minutes

Serves: 3
Nutrition Values
- Calories:- 381
- Carbohydrate:6.3g
- Protein:- 39.1g

- Fat:- 21.5g
- Sugar:- 3.5g
- Sodium:- 0.62g

Ingredients
- 1 pound grass-fed lamb shoulder; trimmed and cut into 2-inch cubes
- 1/2 large green bell pepper; cut into 8 slices
- 1/2 large red bell pepper; cut into 8 slices
- 1/2 cup bone broth
- 3/4 tbsp. olive oil
- 1 celery stalk; chopped
- 1 cup fresh tomatoes; chopped finely
- 1 ½ tbsp. fresh lemon juice
- 1/2 tsp. salt
- 1/2 tsp. black pepper
- 1/2 small onion; chopped.
- 1/2 tbsp. garlic; minced
- 1/2 tsp. dried oregano; crushed
- 1/2 tsp. dried basil; crushed

Directions:
1. Turn the instant pot to the *Sauté* function and heat the oil.
2. Add the garlic and onion and cook for 2 minutes,
3. Stir in all the remaining Ingredients except the bell peppers,
4. Secure the lid and cook for 15 minutes on *Manual* function at high pressure,
5. Natural release the steam for 10 minutes then remove the lid.
6. Stir in the bell peppers and *Sauté* for 8 minutes, Serve hot.

Amazing Lamb Chops

Preparation Time: 35 minutes

Serves: 2
Nutrition Values
- Calories:- 579
- Carbohydrate:- 14g
- Protein:- 70.1g
- Fat:- 25.5g
- Sugar:- 5.3g
- Sodium:- 0.31g

Ingredients
- 1 pound lamb loin chops
- 1 garlic clove; crushed
- 1/2 cup bone broth
- 1/2 small onion; sliced
- 3/4 cup sugar-free; diced tomatoes
- 1 cup carrots; peeled and sliced
- 1/2 tbsp. cold water
- 3/4 tsp. dried rosemary; crushed
- 1 tbsp. arrowroot starch
- 1 ½ tbsp. butter
- Salt and black pepper (to taste

Directions:
1. Add butter to the instant pot and heat it on the *Sauté* function.
2. Place the lamb chops in the pot and cook for 3 minutes each side,

3. Take the chops out of the pot and place them on a plate,
4. Put the onion and garlic into the pot and cook for 3 minutes,
5. Add the remaining Ingredients and secure the lid.
6. Cook on the *Manual* setting for 15 minutes at high pressure,
7. *Quick Release* the steam and remove the lid.
8. Meanwhile; dissolve the arrowroot flour in some water and add the slurry to the pot.
9. Cook for 5 minutes then pour this sauce over the fried chops, Serve hot.

Jamaican Pork Roast Recipe

Preparation Time: 65 minutes

Serves: 6
Nutrition Values
- Calories:- 226
- Carbohydrate:- 0g (Zero gram
- Protein:- 35.4g
- Fat:- 111.7g
- Sugar:- 0g
- Sodium:- 0.13g

Ingredients
- 2 lbs. pork shoulder
- 1/4 cup beef broth
- 3/4 tbsp. olive oil
- 1/4 cup Jamaican jerk spice blend

Directions:
1. Use Jamaican jerk spice with olive oil to marinate the pork for 10 minutes,
2. Select the *Sauté* function on the instant pot and place the marinated pork inside,
3. Sear each side for 4 minutes then add the broth.
4. Secure the lid and cook for 45 minutes at high pressure on the *Manual* setting.
5. Natural release the steam for 10 minutes then remove the lid. Serve hot.

Pork Sausages and Mushrooms

Preparation Time: 55 minutes

Serves: 2
Nutrition Values
- Calories:- 624
- Carbohydrate:- 27.2g
- Protein:- 34.9g
- Fat:- 41.7g
- Sugar:- 7.8g
- Sodium:- 1.95g

Ingredients
- 6 oz. pork sausages
- 2 large Portobello mushrooms
- 1/2 cup whole milk mozzarella cheese; shredded
- 1/4 cup parsley; chopped
- 1/2 cup marinara sauce
- 1/2 cup whole milk ricotta cheese

Directions:
1. Stuff each mushroom with pork sausage,

2. Place the ricotta cheese over the sausages and carve a dent in the center.
3. Drizzle the marinara sauce over the ricotta cheese,
4. Cover with mozzarella cheese on top and place the mushrooms in the instant pot.
5. Secure the lid; select the *Manual* function and cook for 35 minutes at high pressure,
6. Natural release the steam then remove the lid. Serve immediately.

Instant Bacon Lamb Chili

Preparation Time: 60 minutes

Serves: 8
Nutrition Values
- Calories:- 427
- Carbohydrate:- 6.8g
- Protein:- 27.4g
- Fat:- 23g
- Sugar:- 2.3g
- Sodium:- 0.53g

Ingredients
- 8 bacon slices; chopped
- 2 lbs. grass-fed ground lamb
- 1 small onion; chopped.
- 3 tbsp. chili powder
- 2 tbsp. smoked paprika
- 4 tsp. ground cumin
- 2 red bell peppers; seeded and chopped
- 4 garlic cloves; minced
- Freshly ground black pepper to taste

Directions:
1. Set the instant pot to *Sauté* mode and place the bacon inside,
2. Sauté the bacon for 5 minutes then transfer onto a paper towel on a plate,
3. Now add the garlic, onion and bell peppers to the pot and cook for 5 minutes,
4. Add the lamb, spices and cooked bacon to the pot and secure the lid.
5. Use the *Bean/Chili* function to cook for 30 minutes, Natural release the steam then, remove the lid. Serve hot.

Quick Spicy Minced Meat

Preparation Time: 40 minutes

Serves: 2
Nutrition Values
- Calories:- 343
- Carbohydrate:4.8g
- Protein:- 28.7g
- Fat:- 22.5g
- Sugar:- 1.3g
- Sodium:- 0.67g

Ingredients
- 1/2 pound ground lamb meat
- 1/2 cup onion; chopped
- 1/4 tsp. cumin
- 1/4 tsp. cayenne pepper
- 1/2 tbsp. garlic

- 1/2 tbsp. minced ginger
- 1/4 tsp. turmeric
- 1/4 tsp. ground coriander
- 1/2 tsp. salt

Directions:
1. Set the instant pot to *Sauté* mode,
2. Add the onions; garlic and ginger and sauté for 5 minutes,
3. Add the remaining Ingredients to the pot and secure the lid.
4. Cook on the *Manual* function for 15 minutes at high pressure,
5. When it beeps; *Natural Release* the steam for 15 minutes, Remove the lid and serve immediately.

Spicy Pork Ribs

Preparation Time: 1 hour 55 minutes

Serves: 3
Nutrition Values
- Calories:- 852
- Carbohydrate:- 7.3g
- Protein:- 80.7g
- Fat:- 53.8g
- Sugar:- 6.1g
- Sodium:- 0.83g

Ingredients
- 2 lbs. pork ribs
- 3/4 tsp. erythritol
- 1/2 tsp. garlic powder
- 1/4 tsp. coriander powder
- 1/4 cup tomato ketchup
- 3/4 tbsp. red wine vinegar
- 1/2 tsp. ground mustard
- 1/4 tsp. liquid smoke
- 1/2 tsp. all spice
- 1/2 tsp. salt
- 1/4 tsp. black pepper
- 1/2 tsp. onion powder

Directions:
1. Add all the dry spices to the pork and marinate for 1 hour.
2. In a separate bowl; combine the vinegar, mustard, ketchup and liquid smoke to prepare a sauce,
3. Place the marinated ribs in the instant pot and pour the sauce over it.
4. Secure the lid and select the *Manual* function. Cook for 35 minutes at high pressure,
5. Natural release the steam for 5 minutes then remove the lid.
6. Transfer the ribs to a platter.
7. Cook the remaining sauce in the pot on the *Sauté* setting for 5 minutes, To serve; drizzle the sauce over the ribs,

Fish & seafood

Shrimp and Parsley Mix

Preparation time: 5 minutes
Cooking time: 4 minutes

Serves: 4

Ingredients:
- 1 and ½ pounds shrimp, peeled and deveined
- A pinch of salt and black pepper
- 1 tablespoon parsley, chopped
- 2 tablespoons tomato sauce
- ½ tablespoon sweet paprika, chopped
- 2 garlic cloves, minced

Directions:
In your instant pot, combine the shrimp with the rest of the ingredients, put the lid on and cook on High for 4 minutes.
Release the pressure fast for 5 minutes, divide the mix into bowls and serve.

Nutrition Value: calories 232, fat 7, fiber 3, carbs 7, protein 9

Cod and Cauliflower Rice

Preparation time: 5 minutes
Cooking time: 12 minutes

Serves: 4

Ingredients:
- 4 cod fillets, boneless
- A pinch of salt and black pepper
- 1 cup cauliflower, riced
- 1 cup chicken stock
- 2 tablespoons tomato puree
- 1 tablespoon cilantro, chopped

Directions:
In your instant pot, combine all the ingredients, put the lid on and cook on High for 12 minutes.
Release the pressure fast for 5 minutes, divide the mix between plates and serve.

Nutrition Value: calories 232, fat 9, fiber 2, carbs 6, protein 8

Salmon And Baby Carrots

Preparation time: 10 minutes
Cooking time: 12 minutes

Serves: 4

Ingredients:
- 4 salmon fillets, boneless
- ½ cup veggie stock

- 2 garlic cloves, minced
- 1 red onion, minced
- 1 tablespoon avocado oil
- 2 cups baby carrots, trimmed
- A pinch of salt and black pepper
- 1 tablespoon rosemary, chopped

Directions:
Set the instant pot on Sauté mode, add the oil, heat it up, add the onion and garlic and sauté for 2 minutes.
Add the rest of the ingredients, put the lid on and cook on High for 10 minutes.
Release the pressure naturally for 10 minutes, divide the salmon and carrots mix between plates and serve.

Nutrition Value: calories 200, fat 13, fiber 3, carbs 6, protein 11

Spicy Trout

Preparation time: 5 minutes
Cooking time: 10 minutes

Serves: 4

Ingredients:
- 4 trout fillets, boneless
- 2 tablespoons chili pepper, minced
- Juice of 1 lime
- ½ cup veggie stock
- A pinch of salt and black pepper
- A pinch of cayenne pepper
- 1 tablespoon chives, chopped

Directions:
In your instant pot, mix the trout fillets with the rest of the ingredients except the chives, put the lid on and cook on High for 10 minutes.
Release the pressure fast for 5 minutes, arrange the trout between plates, sprinkle the chives on top and serve with a side salad.

Nutrition Value: calories 200, fat 12, fiber 2, carbs 6, protein 9

Thyme Cod and Tomatoes

Preparation time: 10 minutes
Cooking time: 15 minutes

Serves: 4

Ingredients:
- 4 cod fillets, boneless
- 1 red onion, chopped
- 3 tomatoes, roughly chopped
- 2 tablespoons thyme, chopped
- 3 tablespoons olive oil
- A pinch of salt and black pepper
- 2 tablespoons tomato puree

Directions:

Set the instant pot on Sauté mode, add the oil, heat it up, add the onion, salt and pepper, toss and cook for 2 minutes.
Add the cod and the rest of the ingredients, put the lid on and cook on High for 10 minutes.
Release the pressure naturally for 10 minutes, divide the whole mix between plates and serve.

Nutrition Value: calories 200, fat 12, fiber 2, carbs 5, protein 6

Salmon Cakes and Sauce

Preparation time: 10 minutes
Cooking time: 12 minutes

Serves: 4

Ingredients:
- 1 teaspoon olive oil
- 1 egg, whisked
- 1 pound salmon meat, minced
- 2 tablespoons lemon zest, grated
- 1 teaspoon lemon juice
- A pinch of salt and black pepper
- 1 cup tomato sauce

Directions:
In a bowl, combine the salmon with the egg and the rest of the ingredients except the tomato sauce and the oil, stir well and shape medium cakes out of this mix.
Set the instant pot on Sauté mode, add the oil, heat it up, add the salmon cakes and cook them for 2 minutes on each side.
Add the tomato sauce, put the lid on and cook on High for 8 minutes.
Release the pressure naturally for 10 minutes, divide the mix between plates and serve.

Nutrition Value: calories 192, fat 9, fiber 2, carbs 8, protein 7

Sea Bass and Artichokes

Preparation time: 10 minutes
Cooking time: 15 minutes

Serves: 4

Ingredients:
- 1 pound sea bass, skinless, boneless and cubed
- 1 yellow onion, chopped
- 12 ounces canned artichokes, roughly chopped
- 1 and ½ cups coconut cream
- A pinch of salt and black pepper
- 1 tablespoon cilantro, chopped

Directions:
In your instant pot, combine the sea bass with the rest of the ingredients except the cilantro, put the lid on and cook on High for 15 minutes.
Release the pressure naturally for 10 minutes, divide the mix into bowls, sprinkle the cilantro on top and serve.

Nutrition Value: calories 210, fat 9, fiber 2, carbs 6, protein 7

Cod and Strawberries Sauce

Preparation time: 5 minutes
Cooking time: 15 minutes

Serves: 4

Ingredients:
- 6 cod fillets, boneless
- 2 tablespoons olive oil
- 2 shallots, minced
- 2 garlic cloves, minced
- 2 tablespoons parsley, chopped
- 1 cup strawberries, chopped
- 2 tablespoons lemon juice
- A pinch of salt and black pepper
- 2 tablespoons balsamic vinegar

Directions:
Set the instant pot on Sauté mode, add the oil, heat it up, add the shallots and the garlic and sauté for 2 minutes.
Add the berries, vinegar, salt and pepper, toss, and cook for 2 minutes more.
Add the fish, put the lid on and cook on High for 10 minutes.
Release the pressure fast for 5 minutes, divide the mix between plates, sprinkle the parsley on top, drizzle the lemon juice all over and serve.

Nutrition Value: calories 200, fat 10, fiber 2, carbs 5, protein 9

Tilapia and Lemon Sauce

Preparation time: 10 minutes
Cooking time: 20 minutes

Serves: 4

Ingredients:
- 1 pound tilapia fillets, boneless and cubed
- 2 tablespoons parsley, chopped
- 2 tablespoons lemon juice
- 1 teaspoon lemon zest, grated
- 2 garlic cloves, minced
- 1 shallot, chopped
- 1 tablespoon avocado oil
- ½ pint coconut cream
- A pinch of salt and black pepper

Directions:
Set the instant pot on Sauté mode, add the oil, heat it up, add the garlic and the shallot and cook for 2 minutes.
Add the tilapia and the remaining ingredients, put the lid on and cook on Low for 15 minutes.
Release the pressure naturally for 10 minutes, divide everything between plates and serve.

Nutrition Value: calories 200, fat 13, fiber 3, carbs 6, protein 11

Shrimp and Chicken Mix

Preparation time: 5 minutes
Cooking time: 10 minutes

Serves: 4

Ingredients:
- 1 pound chicken breast, skinless, boneless and cubed
- 1 pound shrimp, peeled and deveined
- 2 tablespoons olive oil
- 2 tablespoons garlic, chopped
- 2 cups red bell peppers, chopped
- 1 and ½ cups chicken stock
- 1 tablespoon Creole seasoning
- 1 cup tomatoes, crushed
- 1 tablespoon parsley, chopped

Directions:
Set your instant pot on Sauté mode, add the oil, heat it up, add the garlic and the bell peppers and sauté for 2 minutes.
Add the shrimp and the rest of the ingredients except the parsley, put the lid on and cook on High for 8 minutes.
Release the pressure fast for 5 minutes, divide the mix between plates and serve with the parsley sprinkled on top.

Nutrition Value: calories 211, fat 12, fiber 3, carbs 6, protein 7

Tuna and Tomatoes

Preparation time: 10 minutes
Cooking time: 10 minutes

Serves: 4

Ingredients:
- ½ cup red onion, chopped
- 1 tablespoon olive oil
- 14 ounces canned tomatoes, chopped
- 1 tablespoon oregano, chopped
- A pinch of salt and black pepper
- 14 ounces tuna fillets, boneless, skinless and cubed
- 1 tablespoon parsley, chopped

Directions:
Set your instant pot on Sauté mode, add the oil, heat it up, add the onion and sauté for 2 minutes.
Add the tomatoes, oregano, salt and pepper, stir and cook for 2 minutes more.
Add the tuna, put the lid on and cook on High for 6 minutes.
Release the pressure naturally for 10 minutes, divide the mix between plates, sprinkle the parsley on top and serve.

Nutrition Value: calories 200, fat 12, fiber 2, carbs 6, protein 13

Simple Fish Tacos

Serves:2
Preparation Time: 8 minutes
Ingredients:

- 2 tilapia fillets
- 1/4 cup fresh cilantro, chopped
- 1 fresh lime juice
- 2 tbsp paprika
- 1 tsp olive oil
- Pinch of salt

Directions for Cooking:
1. Place fish fillets in the middle of the parchment paper piece.
2. Drizzle fish fillet with oil and lime juice. Season with paprika and salt.
3. Sprinkle chopped cilantro on top of fish fillet.
4. Fold parchment paper around the fish fillet and make a packet.
5. Pour 1 1/2 cups of water into the instant pot then place a trivet in the pot.
6. Place parchment paper packet on top of the trivet.
7. Seal pot with lid and cook on high pressure for 8 minutes.
8. Release pressure using quick release method than open the lid.
9. Serve and enjoy.

Nutrition Value:

Calories: 186; Carbohydrates: 5.8g; Protein: 33.2g; Fat: 5.2g; Sugar: 1.1g; Sodium: 141mg

Balsamic Salmon

Serves:2
Preparation Time: 3 minutes
Ingredients:

- 2 salmon fillets
- 1 cup water
- 2 tbsp balsamic vinegar
- 2 tbsp honey
- Pepper
- Salt

Directions for Cooking:
1. Season salmon fish fillets with pepper and salt.
2. In a small bowl, mix together vinegar and honey. Brush on top of fish fillets.
3. Pour water into the instant pot then place trivet into the pot.
4. Place seasoned fish fillets skin side down on top of the trivet.
5. Seal pot with lid and cook on high pressure for 3 minutes.
6. Release pressure using quick release method then open the lid.
7. Remove fish fillets on serving the dish and garnish with parsley.
8. Serve and enjoy.

Nutrition Value:

Calories: 303; Carbohydrates: 17.5g; Protein: 34.6g; Fat: 11g; Sugar: 17.3g; Sodium: 34.6mg

Shrimp Gumbo

Serves: 4
Preparation Time: 25 minutes
Ingredients:
- 1 lb shrimp, peeled and deveined
- 1 bay leaf
- 2/3 cup chicken stock
- 14.5 oz can tomatoes, drained and diced
- 2 tbsp creole seasoning
- 1 onion, diced
- 2 celery ribs, diced
- 1 bell pepper, diced
- 12 oz andouille sausage, sliced
- 2 tbsp olive oil
- Pepper
- Salt

Directions for Cooking:
1. Add oil into the instant pot and set pot on sauté mode.
2. Add sausage into the pot and sauté until brown, about 2-3 minutes.
3. Remove sausage from pot and place on a plate.
4. Add pepper, seasoning, onion, and celery to the pot and sauté for 1-2 minutes.
5. Return sausage to the pot with stock, bay leaf, and tomatoes. Stir well.
6. Seal pot with lid and cook on high pressure for 5 minutes.
7. Allow to release pressure naturally for 5 minutes then release using quick release method.
8. Set pot on sauté mode. Add shrimp and sauté for 3-4 minutes. Season with pepper and salt.
9. Serve and enjoy.

Nutrition Value:

Calories: 531; Carbohydrates: 15.6g; Protein: 43.7g; Fat: 32.4g; Sugar: 7g; Sodium: 3310mg

Quick Garlic Mussels

Serves: 4
Preparation Time: 6 minutes
Ingredients:
- 2 lbs mussels, cleaned
- 1/2 cup white wine
- 1/2 cup chicken broth
- 3 garlic cloves, minced
- 2 shallots, chopped
- 2 tbsp butter

Directions for Cooking:
1. Add butter to the instant pot and set the pot on sauté mode.
2. Add onion to the pot and sauté until softened
3. Add garlic and sauté for 1 minute.
4. Add remaining ingredients and stir well.
5. Seal pot with lid and cook on high for 5 minutes.
6. Allow to release pressure naturally then open the lid.
7. Stir well and serve.

Nutrition Value:

Calories: 279; Carbohydrates: 10g; Protein: 27.8g; Fat: 11g; Sugar: 0.3g; Sodium: 787mg

Shrimp Risotto

Serves: 6
Preparation Time: 16 minutes
Ingredients:
- 1 1/2 cups arborio rice
- 1/4 cup parmesan cheese, grated
- 3/4 lb shrimp, cooked
- 1 cup asparagus, chopped
- 1 tbsp butter
- 3 1/2 cups chicken stock
- 1/2 cup white wine
- 1 cup cremini mushrooms, sliced
- 1 small onion, diced
- 2 tsp olive oil
- 1/2 tsp pepper
- Salt

Directions for Cooking:
1. Add oil into the instant pot and set pot on sauté mode.
2. Add onion to the pot and sauté for 2-3 minutes.
3. Add mushrooms and cook for 4-5 minutes.
4. Add rice and sauté until lightly brown.
5. Add stock and wine and stir well.
6. Seal pot with lid and cook on high for 6 minutes,
7. Release pressure using quick release method than open the lid.
8. Set pot on sauté mode. Add asparagus and butter and sauté for 1 minute.
9. Add shrimp and cook until shrimp are pink, about 1 minute.
10. Add cheese and stir until cheese melted.
11. Serve and enjoy.

Nutrition Value:

Calories: 329; Carbohydrates: 42.2g; Protein: 19.4g; Fat: 6.6g; Sugar: 1.7g; Sodium: 731mg

Basil Tomato Tilapia

Serves: 4
Preparation Time: 4 minutes
Ingredients:
- 4 tilapia fillets
- 2 tbsp olive oil
- 1/4 cup basil, chopped
- 2 garlic cloves, minced
- 3 tomatoes, chopped
- 1/8 tsp pepper
- 1/4 tsp salt

Directions for Cooking:
1. Pour half cup of water into the instant pot.
2. Add fish fillets into the instant pot steamer basket and season with pepper and salt.
3. Seal pot with lid and cook on high pressure for 2 minutes.
4. Release pressure using quick release method than open the lid.
5. In a bowl, mix together tomatoes, oil, garlic, vinegar, pepper, and salt.
6. Place cooked fish fillets on serving dish and top with tomato mixture.

7. Serve and enjoy.

Nutrition Value:

Calories: 219; Carbohydrates: 4.2g; Protein: 33g; Fat: 9.2g; Sugar: 2.5g; Sodium: 212mg

Shrimp Herb Risotto
Serves:4
Preparation Time: 17 minutes
Ingredients:

- 1 lb shrimp, peeled, deveined, and chopped
- 1/2 cup parmesan cheese, grated
- 1 cup clam juice
- 3 cups chicken stock
- 1/4 cup dry sherry
- 1 1/2 cups Arborio rice
- 1 tbsp sweet paprika
- 1 tbsp oregano, minced
- 1 red pepper, chopped
- 1 onion, chopped
- 2 tbsp butter
- 1/2 tsp pepper
- 1/2 tsp salt

Directions for Cooking:
1. Add butter into the instant pot and set the pot on sauté mode.
2. Add onion and pepper and sauté until onion is softened.
3. Add paprika, oregano, pepper, and salt. Stir for minute.
4. Add rice and stir for a minute. Add sherry, clam juice, and stock. Stir well.
5. Seal pot with lid and cook on high pressure for 10 minutes.
6. Release pressure using quick release method than open the lid.
7. Set pot on sauté mode.
8. Add shrimp and cook for 2 minutes.
9. Add cheese and stir until cheese is melted.
10. Serve and enjoy.

Nutrition Value:

Calories: 583; Carbohydrates: 72.2g; Protein: 38.5g; Fat: 13.6g; Sugar: 5.4g; Sodium: 1707mg

Tuna Cheese Noodles

Serves:6
Preparation Time: 4 minutes
Ingredients:

- 3 cups water
- 4 oz cheddar cheese, shredded
- 28 oz can cream of mushroom soup
- 1 cup frozen peas
- 16 oz egg noodles
- 1 can tuna, drained

Directions for Cooking:
1. Add noodles and water into the instant pot.
2. Add cream of mushroom soup, peas, and tuna on top of noodles.
3. Seal pot with lid and cook on high for 4 hours.
4. Release pressure using quick release method than open the lid.

5. Add cheese and stir well.
6. Serve and enjoy.

Nutrition Value:

Calories: 325; Carbohydrates: 33.8g; Protein: 19g; Fat: 12.5g; Sugar: 4.5g; Sodium: 665mg

Soup & Stews

Ginger Cod Soup

Preparation time: 6 minutes
Cooking time: 15 minutes

Serves: 4

Ingredients:
- 1 yellow onion, chopped
- 1 pound cod fillets, boneless, skinless and cubed
- 12 cups chicken stock
- 1 carrot, sliced
- 1 celery stalk, chopped
- 1 tablespoon olive oil
- A pinch of salt and black pepper
- 2 tablespoons ginger, grated

Directions:
Set your instant pot on sauté mode, add oil, heat it up, add the onion, carrot, celery and ginger, stir and sauté for 4 minutes.
Add the rest of the ingredients, put the lid on and cook on High for 10 minutes.
Release the pressure fast for 6 minutes, ladle into bowls and serve.

Nutrition Value: calories 201, fat 8, fiber 2, carbs 5, protein 9

Potato and Parsley Cream

Preparation time: 5 minutes
Cooking time: 20 minutes

Serves: 4

Ingredients:
- 6 cups gold potatoes, cubed
- 2 tablespoons olive oil
- ½ cup yellow onion, chopped
- 6 cups chicken stock
- A pinch of salt and black pepper
- 2 tablespoons parsley, chopped
- 2 cups coconut cream
- 1 cup cheddar cheese, grated

Directions:
Set your instant pot on Sauté mode, add the oil, heat it up, add the onion, stir and sauté 5 minutes

Add the potatoes, stock, salt and pepper, put the lid on and cook on High for 10 minutes. Release the pressure fast for 5 minutes, add the cream, and blend the soup using an immersion blender. Set the pot on Sauté mode, add the cheese and parsley, cook the soup for 3 minutes more, divide into bowls and serve.

Nutrition Value: calories 210, fat 7, fiber 4, carbs 6, protein 11

Corn and Zucchini Soup

Preparation time: 10 minutes
Cooking time: 15 minutes

Serves: 4

Ingredients:
- 1 tablespoon olive oil
- 1 celery stalk, chopped
- 1 yellow onion, chopped
- 2 cups corn
- 2 zucchinis, cubed
- 2 cups tomatoes, chopped
- 4 garlic cloves, minced
- 30 ounces chicken stock, low-sodium
- A pinch of salt and black pepper
- 2 tablespoons basil, chopped

Directions:
Set your instant pot on Sauté mode, add the oil, heat it up, add the onion, stir and sauté for 5 minutes. Add the rest of the ingredients except the basil, stir, put the lid on and cook on High for 10 minutes. Release the pressure naturally for 10 minutes, add the basil, divide the soup into bowls.

Nutrition Value: calories 185, fat 6, fiber 4, carbs 8, protein 10

Bell Pepper and Tomato Soup

Preparation time: 10 minutes
Cooking time: 20 minutes

Serves: 4

Ingredients:
- 1 yellow onion, chopped
- 2 tablespoons olive oil
- 2 red bell peppers, roughly chopped
- 1 pound tomatoes, cubed
- 3 tablespoons tomato paste
- 2 celery ribs, chopped
- 6 cups chicken stock
- 1 teaspoon garlic powder
- ½ tablespoon basil, dried
- ½ teaspoon red pepper flakes

Directions:
Set the instant pot on Sauté mode, add the oil, heat it up, add the onion, garlic powder, basil and the pepper flakes, stir and sauté for 5 minutes.
Add the rest of the ingredients, put the lid on and cook on High for 15 minutes.
Release the pressure naturally for 10 minutes, divide the soup into bowls and serve.

Nutrition Value: calories 180, fat 5, fiber 3, carbs 6, protein 10

Carrots and Cabbage Soup

Preparation time: 10 minutes
Cooking time: 10 minutes

Serves: 4

Ingredients:
- 1 green cabbage head, shredded
- A pinch of salt and black pepper
- ½ pound carrots, sliced
- 1 yellow onion, chopped
- 2 tablespoons olive oil
- 3 garlic cloves, minced
- ¼ cup cilantro, chopped
- 4 cups chicken stock

Directions:
1. In your instant pot, combine all the ingredients, put the lid on and cook on High for 10 minutes.
2. Release the pressure naturally for 10 minutes, ladle the soup into bowls and serve.

Nutrition Value: calories 172, fat 4, fiber 4, carbs 6, protein 9

Salsa Turkey Soup

Preparation time: 10 minutes
Cooking time: 20 minutes

Serves: 4

Ingredients:
- 1 turkey breast, skinless, boneless and cubed
- 2 tablespoons olive oil
- 1 yellow onion, chopped
- 3 garlic cloves, minced
- 16 ounces chunky salsa
- 30 ounces chicken stock
- A pinch of salt and black pepper
- 1 tablespoon parsley, chopped
- 1 tablespoon chili powder

Directions:
Set your instant pot on Sauté mode, add the oil, heat it up, add the onion and garlic, stir and cook 5 minutes.
Add the meat and brown for 2 minutes more.
Add the rest of the ingredients, put the lid on and cook on High for 13 minutes.
Release the pressure naturally for 10 minutes, divide the soup into bowls and serve.

Nutrition Value: calories 200, fat 4, fiber 4, carbs 7, protein 17

Tarragon Corn Soup

Preparation time: 10 minutes
Cooking time: 15 minutes

Serves: 4

Ingredients:
- 2 tablespoons olive oil
- 1 yellow onion, chopped
- 2 garlic cloves, minced
- 3 cups corn
- 4 tarragon springs, chopped
- 1 quart chicken stock
- A pinch of salt and black pepper
- 1 tablespoon chives, chopped

Directions:
Set your instant pot on Sauté mode, add the oil, heat it up, add the onion and the garlic, stir and sauté for 5 minutes.
Add the rest of the ingredients except the chives, put the lid on and cook on High for 10 minutes.
Release the pressure naturally for 10 minutes, ladle the soup into bowls, sprinkle the chives on top and serve.

Nutrition Value: calories 200, fat 5, fiber 4, carbs 8, protein 11

Zucchini and Chicken Soup

Preparation time: 10 minutes
Cooking time: 15 minutes

Serves: 4

Ingredients:
- 2 zucchinis, cubed
- ½ cup green onions, chopped
- 2 tablespoons olive oil
- ½ cup celery, chopped
- 29 ounces canned chicken stock
- 1 garlic clove, minced
- 2 cups tomatoes, cubed
- A pinch of salt and black pepper
- 2 chicken breasts, skinless, boneless and cubed
- 1 tablespoon parsley, chopped

Directions:
Set your instant pot on Sauté mode, add the green onions, garlic, celery and tomatoes, toss and cook for 3 minutes.
Add the rest of the ingredients except the parsley, put the lid on and cock on High for 12 minutes.

Release the pressure naturally for 10 minutes, ladle the soup into bowls, sprinkle the parsley on top and serve.

Nutrition Value: calories 192, fat 8, fiber 4, carbs 9, protein 12

Bacon Corn Soup

Preparation time: 10 minutes
Cooking time: 12 minutes

Serves: 4

Ingredients:
- 6 cups corn
- 2 tablespoons avocado oil
- ½ cup yellow onion, chopped
- 28 ounces canned chicken stock
- A pinch of salt and black pepper
- 3 ounces cream cheese, cubed
- 2 cups coconut cream
- 1 cup cheddar cheese, shredded
- 6 bacon slices, cooked and crumbled

Directions:
Set your instant pot on Sauté mode, add the oil, heat it up, add the onion, stir and cook 5 minutes
Add the rest of the ingredients except the cheddar, cream cheese and bacon, put the lid on and cook on High for 10 minutes.
Release the pressure naturally for 10 minutes, add the cheddar and cream cheese and blend the soup using an immersion blender.
Divide the soup into bowls, sprinkle the bacon on top and serve.

Nutrition Value: calories 182, fat 3, fiber 4, carbs 6, protein 12

Chicken and Pea Soup

Preparation time: 10 minutes
Cooking time: 20 minutes

Serves: 4

Ingredients:
- 2 tablespoons olive oil
- 1 pound chicken breasts, skinless, boneless and cubed
- 1 yellow onion, chopped
- ½ cup carrots, chopped
- 2 garlic cloves, minced
- 28 ounces chicken stock
- A pinch of salt and black pepper
- 1 pound fresh peas
- ½ cup coconut cream
- 1 tablespoon dill, chopped

Directions:
Set the instant pot on Sauté mode, add the oil, heat it up, add the chicken, onion and garlic and brown for 4 minutes.
Add the rest of the ingredients except the cream and dill, put the lid on and cook on High for 12 minutes.
Release the pressure naturally for 10 minutes, set the pot on Sauté mode again, add the cream and dill, cook for 4 minutes more, ladle into bowls and serve.

Nutrition Value: calories 192, fat 5, fiber 3, carbs 7, protein 16

Beef and Tomato Soup

Preparation time: 10 minutes
Cooking time: 20 minutes

Serves: 4

Ingredients:
- 1 pound beef stew meat, cubed
- 3 garlic cloves, minced
- 1 yellow onion, chopped
- 1 tablespoon olive oil
- 28 ounces beef stock
- 1 pound tomatoes, peeled and chopped
- 1 cup tomato sauce
- A pinch of salt and black pepper
- 1 tablespoon parsley, chopped

Directions:
Set your instant pot on Sauté mode, add the oil, heat it up, add the meat and brown for 3 minutes.
Add garlic and onion, stir and cook for 2 minutes more.
Add the rest of the ingredients except the parsley, put the lid on and cook on High for 15 minutes.
Release the pressure naturally for 10 minutes, add the parsley, ladle the soup into bowls and serve.

Nutrition Value: calories 261, fat 6, fiber 4, carbs 6, protein 15

Chicken and Eggplant Soup

Preparation time: 10 minutes
Cooking time: 15 minutes
SmartPoints: 5

Ingredients:
- 1 yellow onion, chopped
- 1 tablespoon olive oil
- 1 celery rib, chopped
- 1 eggplant, cubed
- A pinch of salt and black pepper
- 6 cups chicken stock
- 2 chicken breasts, skinless, boneless and cubed
- 1 tablespoon parsley, chopped

Directions:

Set your instant pot on Sauté mode, add the oil, heat it up, add the onion and celery, stir and cook for 3 minutes.
Add the rest of the ingredients except the parsley, put the lid on and cook on High for 12 minutes.
Release the pressure naturally for 10 minutes, add the parsley, ladle into bowls and serve.

Nutrition Value: calories 200, fat 4, fiber 3, carbs 6, protein 12

Turmeric Kale Stew

Preparation time: 5 minutes
Cooking time: 12 minutes
SmartPoints: 3

Ingredients:
- 1 yellow onion, chopped
- 2 teaspoons olive oil
- 2 carrots, chopped
- 2 garlic cloves, minced
- 1 teaspoon turmeric powder
- A pinch of salt and black pepper
- 6 cups kale, torn
- 2 cups veggie stock
- 1 cup tomato puree

Directions:
Set your instant pot on Sauté mode, add the oil, heat it up, add onion, garlic and carrots, stir and sauté for 2 minutes.
Add the rest of the ingredients, put the lid on and cook on High for 10 minutes.
Release the pressure fast for 5 minutes, divide the stew into bowls and serve.

Nutrition Value: calories 172, fat 4, fiber 4, carbs 7, protein 8

Zucchini and Cabbage Stew

Preparation time: 10 minutes
Cooking time: 15 minutes

Serves: 4

Ingredients:
- 2 tablespoons olive oil
- 2 zucchinis, sliced
- A pinch of salt and black pepper
- 1 small yellow onion, chopped
- 1 red chili, chopped
- 1 green cabbage head, shredded
- 2 tablespoons tomato sauce
- ¼ cup veggie stock
- 1 teaspoon sweet paprika

Directions:
Set your instant pot on Sauté mode, add the oil, heat it up, the onion, chili and the paprika, stir and sauté for 5 minutes.
Add the rest of the ingredients, put the lid on and cook on High for 15 minutes.

Release the pressure naturally for 10 minutes, divide the stew into bowls and serve.

Nutrition Value: calories 165, fat 5, fiber 3, carbs 9, protein 5

Chicken and Cranberries Stew

Preparation time: 10 minutes
Cooking time: 25 minutes

Serves: 4

Ingredients:
- 1 tablespoon avocado oil
- 1 yellow onion, chopped
- 3 celery stalks, chopped
- A pinch of salt and black pepper
- 3 cups chicken meat, cooked and shredded
- 1 cup cranberries, dried
- 15 ounces canned tomatoes, chopped
- 5 cups chicken stock
- 1 tablespoon cilantro, chopped

Directions:
Set your instant pot on Sauté mode, add the oil, heat it up, add the onion and celery, stir and sauté for 5 minutes.
Add the rest of the ingredients, put the lid on and cook on Low for 20 minutes..
Release the pressure naturally for 10 minutes, divide the stew into bowls and serve.

Nutrition Value: calories 200, fat 12, fiber 4, carbs 8, protein 12

Mushroom and Carrots Stew

Preparation time: 10 minutes
Cooking time: 25 minutes

Serves: 6

Ingredients:
- 1 tablespoon olive oil
- 1 red onion, chopped
- 1 teaspoon rosemary, chopped
- 1 and ½ cups chicken stock
- A pinch of salt and black pepper
- ¼ pound white mushrooms, sliced
- 4 carrots, chopped

Directions:
Set your instant pot on Sauté mode, add the oil, heat it up, add the onion and the mushrooms and sauté for 5 minutes.
Add the remaining ingredients, put the lid on and cook on Low for 20 minutes.
Release the pressure naturally for 10 minutes, divide the stew into bowls and serve.

Nutrition Value: **calories 182, fat 4, fiber 4, carbs 8, protein 12**

Artichokes and Beef Stew

Preparation time: 10 minutes
Cooking time: 20 minutes

Serves: 4

Ingredients:
- 1 and ½ pounds beef stew meat, cubed
- 1 tablespoon avocado oil
- 1 yellow onion, chopped
- A pinch of salt and black pepper
- 3 carrots, chopped
- 2 garlic cloves, minced
- 10 ounces canned artichokes, drained and chopped
- 1 cup tomatoes, chopped
- 1 cup beef stock
- 1 tablespoon parsley, chopped

Directions:
Set the instant pot on Sauté mode, add the oil, heat it up, add the beef and brown for 3 minutes.
Add the rest of the ingredients except the parsley, put the lid on and cook on High for 17 minutes.
Release the pressure naturally for 10 minutes, add the parsley, divide the stew into bowls and serve.

Nutrition Value: calories 231, fat 13, fiber 3, carbs 8, protein 12

Greek Lamb Stew

Preparation time: 10 minutes
Cooking time: 30 minutes

Serves: 4

Ingredients:
- 2 pounds lamb shoulder, cubed
- 1 tablespoon garlic, minced
- 14 ounces canned tomatoes, chopped
- 2 yellow onions, chopped
- 1 tablespoon olive oil
- 1 teaspoon oregano, dried
- 1 teaspoon basil, dried
- A pinch of salt and black pepper
- ½ cup parsley, chopped

Directions:
Set the pot on Sauté mode, add the oil, heat it up, add the onions, garlic and the meat, stir and brown for 5 minutes.
Add the rest of the ingredients except the parsley, put the lid on and cook on High for 25 minutes.
Release the pressure naturally for 10 minutes, add the parsley, divide the stew into bowls and serve.

Nutrition Value: calories 242, fat 12, fiber 4, carbs 9, protein 15

Lamb and Green Beans Stew

Preparation time: 10 minutes
Cooking time: 20 minutes

Serves: 4

Ingredients:
- 1 yellow onion, chopped
- 1 and ½ pounds lamb shoulder, cubed
- A pinch of salt and black pepper
- ½ pound green beans, trimmed and halved
- 2 cups chicken stock
- 2 carrots, chopped
- ¼ cup parsley, minced

Directions:
In your instant pot, combine all the ingredients except the parsley, put the lid on and cook on High for 20 minutes.
Release the pressure fast for 6 minutes, divide the stew into bowls and serve.

Nutrition Value: calories 251, fat 13, fiber 5, carbs 9, protein 15

Beans, Grains, Rice & pasta

Flavorful Italian Black Beans

Serves: 12
Preparation Time: 45 minutes
Ingredients:

- 1 lb dried black beans, rinsed and drained
- ¼ cup coconut milk
- 4 cups water
- 2 vegetable bouillons
- ¼ tsp cayenne pepper
- ¼ tsp allspice
- 1 tsp Italian seasoning
- 1 tsp thyme
- ¼ bell pepper, diced
- 2 garlic cloves, minced
- 1 onion, chopped
- 1 tbsp olive oil
- ½ tsp salt

Directions for Cooking:
1. Add olive oil into the instant pot and set the pot on sauté mode.
2. Add garlic, onion, vegetable bouillon, cayenne pepper, allspice, Italian seasoning, thyme, and bell pepper and sauté until onion is softened.
3. Add black beans, coconut milk, and water. Stir well.
4. Seal pot with lid and cook on high pressure for 45 minutes.
5. Allow to release pressure naturally for 20 minutes then release using quick release method.
6. Stir well and serve.

Nutrition Value:

Calories: 157; Carbohydrates: 25.2g; Protein: 8.4g; Fat: 3.1g; Sugar: 1.5g; Sodium: 103mg

56. Flavorful White Beans
SmartPoints:
Serves:6
Preparation Time: 30 minutes
Ingredients:
- 1 lb great northern beans, rinsed and drained
- 6 cup vegetable broth
- 1 bay leaf
- 2 tsp garlic powder
- 1 tbsp onion powder
- 1 tsp salt

Directions for Cooking:
1. Add all ingredients into the instant pot and stir well.
2. Seal pot with lid and select bean/chili mode.
3. Allow to release pressure naturally for 20 minutes then release using quick release method.
4. Stir well and serve over rice.

Nutrition Value:

Calories: 302; Carbohydrates: 49.7g; Protein: 21.7g; Fat: 2.3g; Sugar: 3.1g; Sodium: 1162mg

Sweet Maple Baked Beans

Serves:12
Preparation Time: 40 minutes
Ingredients:
- 1 lb dried navy beans, soaked overnight, rinsed, and drained
- 1 cup vegetable stock
- 1 tsp apple cider vinegar
- 1/3 cup maple syrup
- 1 onion, minced
- 2 tsp seasoned salt
- 1 tsp dried mustard
- 8 oz tomato sauce
- 2 cups tomato juice
- 2 cups apple juice

Directions for Cooking:
1. Add all ingredients into the instant pot and stir well.
2. Seal pot with lid and cook on high pressure for 40 minutes.
3. Allow to release pressure naturally then open the lid.
4. Stir well and serve.

Nutrition Value:

Calories: 186; Carbohydrates: 37.4g; Protein: 9.2g; Fat: 1g; Sugar: 13.5g; Sodium: 526mg

58. Tasty Pinto Beans
SmartPoints:
Serves:8
Preparation Time: 25 minutes
Ingredients:
- 1 lb dried pinto beans, soaked overnight, rinsed and drained
- 2 liters water
- 2 tbsp chili powder

- 2 tbsp onion powder
- 3 tbsp garlic powder
- 1 tsp oregano
- 1 tsp salt

Directions for Cooking:
1. Add all ingredients into the instant pot and stir well.
2. Seal pot with lid and cook on manual high pressure for 25 minutes.
3. Allow to release pressure naturally then open the lid.
4. Stir well and serve.

Nutrition Value:

Calories: 220; Carbohydrates: 40.3g; Protein: 13.1g; Fat: 1.1g; Sugar: 2.7g; Sodium: 326mg

Flavors Chipotle Black Beans

Serves:4
Preparation Time: 35 minutes
Ingredients:

- 1 cup dried black beans
- 1 tsp chipotle powder
- 1 tsp paprika
- 2 tsp cumin powder
- 3 cups vegetable broth
- 2 garlic cloves, minced
- ½ onion, diced

Directions for Cooking:
1. Set instant pot on sauté mode.
2. Add onion and garlic to the pot and sauté until onion is softened.
3. Add broth, all spices, and beans to the pot and stir well.
4. Seal pot with lid and select bean/chili mode and set timer for 35 minutes.
5. Allow to release pressure naturally for 15 minutes then release using quick release method.
6. Stir well and serve.

Nutrition Value:

Calories: 207; Carbohydrates: 33.5g; Protein: 14.6g; Fat: 2g; Sugar: 2.2g; Sodium: 578mg

Beans with Tomatillos

Serves:6
Preparation Time: 40 minutes
Ingredients:

- 1 ½ cups dried great northern beans, soaked overnight, rinsed and drained
- 2 tsp dried oregano
- 1 ½ cups water
- 1 ½ tsp ground cumin
- ½ jalapeno pepper, chopped
- 1 cup onion, chopped
- 1 cup poblano, chopped
- 2 cups tomatillos, chopped
- Pepper
- Salt

Directions for Cooking:

1. Add ground cumin, jalapeno pepper, onion, poblano, and tomatillos into the food processor and process until vegetables are in tiny pieces.
2. Pour blended mixture into the instant pot and set the pot on sauté mode and cook for 4 minutes.
3. Add remaining ingredients and stir well to combine.
4. Seal pot with lid and cook on manual high pressure for 35 minutes.
5. Allow to release pressure naturally then open the lid.
6. Stir well and serve.

Nutrition Value:

Calories: 226; Carbohydrates: 44.2g; Protein: 13.5g; Fat: 1.2g; Sugar: 1.9g; Sodium: 40mg

Delicious Beans with Bacon

Serves:8
Preparation Time: 38 minutes
Ingredients:

- 1 lb dried pinto beans
- 2 tbsp hot sauce
- ½ tsp thyme
- 1 tsp garlic powder
- 7 cups vegetable broth
- 2 lbs bacon, cooked and chopped
- ½ tsp black pepper
- 1 tsp sea salt

Directions for Cooking:
1. Add all ingredients into the instant pot and stir well to combine.
2. Seal pot with lid and cook on manual high pressure for 38 minutes.
3. Allow to release pressure naturally for 20 minutes then release using quick release method.
4. Stir well and serve over rice.

Nutrition Value:

Calories: 846; Carbohydrates: 38.3g; Protein: 58.5g; Fat: 49.3g; Sugar: 2g; Sodium: 3623mg

62. Wheat Berry Pilaf
SmartPoints:
Serves:6
Preparation Time: 30 minutes
Ingredients:

- 3 cups water
- 1 ½ cups wheat berries, rinsed and drained
- 2 garlic cloves, minced
- 1 ½ tsp turmeric
- ½ tsp ground coriander
- 1 ½ tsp ground cumin
- ½ cup onion, minced
- 1 tbsp olive oil
- Salt

Directions for Cooking:
1. Add oil into the instant pot and set the pot on sauté mode.
2. Add onion and garlic and sauté until onion softened.
3. Stir in turmeric, coriander, and cumin and sauté for 1-2 minutes.
4. Add wheat berries and sauté for 1-2 minutes.
5. Add water and stir well.

6. Seal pot with lid and cook on manual high pressure for 30 minutes.
7. Allow to release pressure naturally then open the lid.
8. Stir and serve.

Nutrition Value:

Calories: 83; Carbohydrates: 13.3g; Protein: 2.3g; Fat: 2.9g; Sugar: 0.5g; Sodium: 37mg

Healthy Vegetable Quinoa

Serves:4
Preparation Time: 20 minutes
Ingredients:

- 1 ½ cup quinoa, rinsed and drained
- ¼ cup cilantro, chopped
- 1 ½ cups water
- ¼ cup coconut milk
- 1 tsp garam masala
- ½ tsp chili powder
- ½ tsp black pepper
- ¼ tsp turmeric
- 1 carrot, chopped
- 1 cup green beans, chopped
- 1 potato, cubed
- 1 tomato, chopped
- 1 onion, chopped
- 2 tsp ginger paste
- 1 garlic clove, minced
- 1 bay leaf
- 2-star anise
- 3 cloves
- 1 tsp cumin seeds
- 2 tbsp olive oil
- Salt

Directions for Cooking:
1. Add oil into the instant pot and set the pot on sauté mode.
2. Add cumin seeds, cloves, and star anise and sauté for 30 seconds.
3. Add ginger paste, garlic, tomatoes, onions, and all dry spices. Stir well.
4. Add all vegetables, milk, and salt. Stir for 30 seconds.
5. Add quinoa and water. Stir well.
6. Seal pot with lid and cook on manual high pressure for 4 minutes.
7. Allow to release pressure naturally for 10 minutes then release using quick release method.
8. Stir well and serve.

Nutrition Value:

Calories: 403; Carbohydrates: 58.3g; Protein: 11.6g; Fat: 14.8g; Sugar: 3.9g; Sodium: 71mg

Quinoa with Sausage

Serves:4
Preparation Time: 6 minutes
Ingredients:

- 2 cups quinoa, rinsed and drained
- 5 oz mushrooms, halved

- 2 cups broccoli, chopped
- 2 bell peppers, chopped
- 2 cups vegetable stock
- ½ tsp turmeric
- 1 tsp paprika
- 2 tbsp olive oil
- 1 onion, diced
- 1 lb sausage meat

Directions for Cooking:
1. Add oil into the instant pot and set the pot on sauté mode.
2. Add onion and sausage meat and sauté until sausage is lightly browned and cooked.
3. Add turmeric and paprika. Stir well.
4. Add remaining ingredients and stir well.
5. Seal pot with lid and cook on manual high pressure for 1 minute.
6. Allow to release pressure naturally for 10 minutes then release using quick release method.
7. Fluff quinoa with fork and serve.

Nutrition Value:

Calories: 816; Carbohydrates: 66.8g; Protein: 37.4g; Fat: 45.3g; Sugar: 6.1g; Sodium: 1054mg

Chicken Salsa Brown Rice

Serves:4
Preparation Time: 25 minutes

Ingredients:
- 1 cup chicken stock
- 1 cup salsa
- ½ tsp sea salt
- ½ tsp cumin
- 1 tsp chili powder
- 1 cup brown rice
- 1 ½ cups can black beans, rinsed and drained
- 2 chicken breasts, cut into chunks
- 2 garlic cloves, minced
- 1 small onion, diced
- 1 tbsp coconut oil

Directions for Cooking:
1. Add oil into the instant pot and set the pot on sauté mode.
2. Add onion and sauté until softened. Add garlic and cook for a minute. Stir constantly.
3. Add seasonings, beans, brown rice, and chicken. Stir well.
4. Pour stock and salsa and stir well.
5. Seal pot with lid and cook on manual high pressure for 18 minutes.
6. Allow to release pressure naturally then open the lid.
7. Stir well and serve.

Nutrition Value:

Calories: 462; Carbohydrates: 60.3g; Protein: 31.5g; Fat: 10.9g; Sugar: 3.7g; Sodium: 1248mg

Jalapeno Tomato Brown Rice

Serves:3
Preparation Time: 40 minutes
Ingredients:

- 1 cup brown rice
- 1/4 cup tomato paste
- 1 onion, chopped
- 1 tbsp olive oil
- 1 cup water
- 1 jalapeno pepper, sliced
- 2 garlic cloves, minced
- 1/2 tsp salt

Directions for Cooking:
1. Add oil and onion in instant pot and sauté for 3-4 minutes.
2. Add garlic and sauté for a minute.
3. Add brown rice, jalapeno, tomato paste, and salt. Stir well. Pour water and stir.
4. Seal pot with lid and cook on high for 15 minutes.
5. Allow to release pressure naturally for 10 minutes then release using quick release method.
6. Serve and enjoy.

Nutrition Value:

Calories: 306; Carbohydrates: 56.7g; Protein: 6.3g; Fat: 6.6g; Sugar: 4.4g; Sodium: 416mg

Easy Butter Rice

Serves:3
Preparation Time: 25 minutes
Ingredients:

- 1 cup brown rice
- 3/4 cup onion soup
- 4 tbsp butter
- 3/4 cup vegetable broth

Directions for Cooking:
1. Add all ingredients into the instant pot and stir well.
2. Seal pot with lid and cook on high for 15 minutes.
3. Allow to release pressure naturally for 10 minutes then release using quick release method.
4. Stir well and serve.

Nutrition Value:

Calories: 403; Carbohydrates: 52.6g; Protein: 8g; Fat: 18.3g; Sugar: 1.9g; Sodium: 831mg

Tasty Potato Risotto

Serves:4
Preparation Time: 25 minutes
Ingredients:

- 2 cups rice
- 4 cups chicken stock
- 1 medium potato, cubed
- 1 tbsp olive oil
- 1 tbsp tomato paste
- 4 tbsp white wine
- 1 medium onion, chopped
- 1 tsp salt

Directions for Cooking:
1. Add oil into the instant pot and set the pot on sauté mode.

2. Add onion and sauté for 2-3 minutes
3. Add rice and stir for 2 minutes.
4. Add white wine and stir until the rice absorbs wine.
5. Add stock, potatoes, tomato paste, and salt. Stir well.
6. Seal pot with lid and cook on high for 5 minutes.
7. Allow to release pressure naturally for 15 minutes then release using quick release method.
8. Serve and enjoy.

Nutrition Value:

Calories: 445; Carbohydrates: 87.7g; Protein: 8.8g; Fat: 4.8g; Sugar: 3g; Sodium: 1359mg

Garlic Bean Rice

Serves:6
Preparation Time: 50 minutes
Ingredients:
- 2 cups rice
- 2 cups dried black beans, rinsed and drained
- 1 large onion, diced
- 1/2 tbsp olive oil
- 9 cups water
- 3 garlic cloves, minced
- 1 tsp salt

Directions for Cooking:
1. Add oil into the instant pot and set the pot on sauté mode.
2. Add onion and garlic and sauté until onion is softened.
3. Add all remaining ingredients and stir well.
4. Seal pot with lid and cook on high for 27 minutes.
5. Allow to release pressure naturally then open the lid.
6. Stir well and serve.

Nutrition Value:

Calories: 468; Carbohydrates: 92.5g; Protein: 18.8g; Fat: 2.5g; Sugar: 2.5g; Sodium: 406mg

Butter Paprika Rice

Serves:6
Preparation Time: 30 minutes
Ingredients:
- 2 cups rice
- 2 1/2 cups chicken broth
- 2 cubes chicken bouillon
- 3 tsp paprika
- 2 tbsp butter
- 1/4 tsp pepper
- 1 tsp salt

Directions for Cooking:
1. Add all ingredients into the instant pot and stir well.
2. Seal pot with lid and cook on manual high pressure for 7 minutes.
3. Release pressure naturally than open the lid.
4. Fluff rice using the fork.
5. Serve and enjoy.

Nutrition Value:

Calories: 281; Carbohydrates: 50.5g; Protein: 6.8g; Fat: 5.1; Sugar: 0.6g; Sodium: 737mg

Salsa Rice

Serves:4
Preparation Time: 37 minutes
Ingredients:

- 2 cups brown rice
- 1/2 cup salsa
- 2 cups water
- 1 tsp cumin
- 1 tbsp garlic salt

Directions for Cooking:
1. Add all ingredients into the instant pot and stir well.
2. Seal pot with lid and cook on high for 22 minutes.
3. Allow to release pressure naturally for 15 minutes then release using quick release method.
4. Fluff rice with a fork and serve.

Nutrition Value:

Calories: 362; Carbohydrates: 76.2g; Protein: 8.1g; Fat: 2.7g; Sugar: 1.5g; Sodium: 204mg

Saffron Risotto
SmartPoints:
Serves:6
Preparation Time: 25 minutes
Ingredients:

- 1 1/2 cups arborio rice
- 1/2 cup onion, chopped
- 2 tbsp olive oil
- 2 tbsp milk
- 1/2 tsp saffron threads, crushed
- 1 cinnamon stick
- 1/3 cup dried currants
- 1/3 cup almonds, chopped
- 1 tbsp honey
- 3 1/2 cups water
- 1/2 tsp sea salt

Directions for Cooking:
1. Whisk together milk and saffron and set aside.
2. Add oil into the instant pot and set the pot on sauté mode.
3. Add onion and sauté for 5 minutes. Add rice and stir for a minute.
4. Add remaining ingredients into the pot and stir well.
5. Seal pot with lid and cook on high pressure for 5 minutes.
6. Allow to release pressure naturally for 15 minutes then release using quick release method.
7. Stir well and serve.

Nutrition Value:

Calories: 262; Carbohydrates: 43.8g; Protein: 4.7g; Fat: 7.7g; Sugar: 4.2g; Sodium: 167mg

Parmesan Butter Risotto

Serves: 4
Preparation Time: 18 minutes
Ingredients:

- 1 1/2 cups arborio rice
- 1/2 cup parsley, chopped
- 1 onion, diced
- 4 tbsp butter
- 3 tbsp parmesan cheese, grated
- 4 cups chicken broth
- 2 garlic cloves, minced
- 1/4 tsp black pepper
- 1/2 tsp salt

Directions for Cooking:
1. Add butter into the instant pot and set the pot on sauté mode.
2. Add onion and sauté for 5 minutes.
3. Add garlic and rice and stir for 2-3 minutes.
4. Add remaining ingredients and stir well.
5. Seal pot with lid and cook on high for 10 minutes.
6. Release pressure using quick release method than open the lid.
7. Garnish with parsley and serve.

Nutrition Value:

Calories: 441; Carbohydrates: 61.2g; Protein: 12.6g; Fat: 15.1g; Sugar: 2g; Sodium: 1259mg

Squash Mushroom Risotto

Serves: 4
Preparation Time: 38 minutes
Ingredients:

- 1 1/2 cups brown rice
- 1 cup peas
- 3 garlic cloves, minced
- 1/2 cup onion, diced
- 2 tsp olive oil
- 1 tbsp soy sauce
- 1 cup mushrooms, sliced
- 2 cup squash, cubed
- 2 1/2 cups vegetable broth
- Pepper
- Salt

Directions for Cooking:
1. Add olive oil into the instant pot and set the pot on sauté mode.
2. Add onion and garlic into the pot and sauté for a minute.
3. Add remaining ingredients into the pot and stir well.
4. Seal pot with lid and cook on high for 22 minutes.
5. Allow to release pressure naturally for 15 minutes then release using quick release method.
6. Stir well and serve.

Nutrition Value:

Calories: 355; Carbohydrates: 65g; Protein: 12.1g; Fat: 5.4g; Sugar: 4.5g; Sodium: 754mg

Parsley Scallions Risotto

Serves:4
Preparation Time: 11 minutes
Ingredients:
- 1 cup arborio rice
- 1/4 cup parsley, chopped
- 3 scallions, chopped
- 2 cups chicken stock
- 1/8 cup white wine
- 2 tbsp butter
- 1/2 tsp salt

Directions for Cooking:
1. Add butter into the pot and set the pot on sauté mode.
2. Add scallions and parsley and sauté for 2 minutes.
3. Add remaining ingredients and stir well.
4. Seal pot with lid and cook on high for 9 minutes.
5. Release pressure using quick release method than open the lid.
6. Stir well and serve.

Nutrition Value:

Calories: 238; Carbohydrates: 39.4g; Protein: 3.9g; Fat: 6.3g; Sugar: 0.7g; Sodium: 721mg

Cauliflower Risotto

Serves:4
Preparation Time: 14 minutes
Ingredients:
- 1 medium cauliflower head, cut into florets
- 2 tbsp coconut aminos
- 3 garlic cloves, minced
- 1 lb mushrooms, sliced
- 1 small onion, diced
- 2 tbsp tapioca starch
- 1/4 cup nutritional yeast
- 1 cup chicken broth
- 1 cup coconut milk
- 1 tbsp coconut oil
- 1/2 tsp sea salt

Directions for Cooking:
1. Add cauliflower florets into the food processor and process until it looks like rice.
2. Add coconut oil into the instant pot and set the pot on sauté mode.
3. Add garlic, mushrooms, and onion into the pot and sauté for 7 minutes.
4. Add coconut aminos and stir for 5 minutes.
5. Add cauliflower rice, nutritional yeast, broth, coconut milk, and salt. Stir well.
6. Seal pot with lid and cook on high for 2 minutes.
7. Release pressure using quick release method than open the lid.
8. Sprinkle tapioca starch and stir until thickened.
9. Serve and enjoy.

Nutrition Value:

Calories: 300; Carbohydrates: 26.1g; Protein: 13.9g; Fat: 19.1g; Sugar: 8.5g; Sodium: 491mg

Cauliflower Turmeric Rice

Serves:4
Preparation Time: 3 minutes
Ingredients:

- 1 lb cauliflower, cut into florets
- 1/2 tbsp parsley, dried
- 2 tbsp olive oil
- 1/4 tsp cumin
- 1 lime juice
- 1/4 tsp paprika
- 1/4 tsp turmeric
- 4 tbsp cilantro, chopped
- 1/4 tsp salt

Directions for Cooking:
1. Add all cauliflower florets into the steamer basket and place basket into the instant pot.
2. Pour 1 cup water into the instant pot.
3. Seal pot with lid and cook on high for 1 minute.
4. Release pressure using quick release method than open the lid.
5. Transfer cauliflower on a plate.
6. Add olive oil in instant pot and set pot on sauté mode.
7. Add cauliflower florets into the instant pot and using masher break cauliflower into the small pieces.
8. Add turmeric, cumin, paprika, parsley, and salt and sauté for 2 minutes.
9. Add lime juice and serve.

Nutrition Value:

Calories: 90; Carbohydrates: 6.3g; Protein: 2.3g; Fat: 7.2g; Sugar: 2.7g; Sodium: 182mg

Coconut Cauliflower Rice

Serves:4
Preparation Time: 1 minute
Ingredients:

- 16 oz cauliflower rice
- 1 1/2 tsp arrowroot
- 1 cup coconut milk
- 1/2 tsp sea salt

Directions for Cooking:
1. Add coconut milk, cauliflower rice, and sea salt into the instant pot and mix well.
2. Seal pot with lid and cook on high for 1 minute.
3. Release pressure using quick release method than open the lid.
4. Add arrowroot and stir until thickened.
5. Serve and enjoy.

Nutrition Value:

Calories: 167; Carbohydrates: 9.5g; Protein: 3.7g; Fat: 14.4g; Sugar: 4.7g; Sodium: 277mg

Spaghetti Noodles

Serves:2
Preparation Time: 15 minutes
Ingredients:
- 6 oz spaghetti noodles
- 1/2 tsp dried oregano
- 1/2 tsp dried basil
- 1 garlic clove, minced
- 1/2 onion, diced
- 1/2 lb ground beef
- 2 tbsp parmesan cheese
- 1 1/4 cups chicken stock
- 2 tbsp tomato paste
- 1 cup jar spaghetti sauce
- 1 tbsp olive oil
- 1/2 tsp salt

Directions for Cooking:
1. Set instant pot on sauté mode and olive oil into the pot.
2. Add ground beef and sauté for 3 minutes, stir and break meat with a spoon.
3. Add onion and cook for 4 minutes.
4. Stir in garlic, oregano, basil, spaghetti sauce, chicken stock, tomato paste, parmesan cheese, pepper, and salt. Stir well.
5. Turn off the pot. Break noodles in half and add layer them in the meat mixture.
6. Seal instant pot with lid and cook on high for 8 minutes.
7. Release pressure using quick release method than open the lid.
8. Stir well and serve.

Nutrition Value:

Calories: 572; Carbohydrates: 57.5g; Protein: 46.2g; Fat: 17g; Sugar: 5.9g; Sodium: 1468mg

Polenta with Grape Tomatoes

Serves: 4
Preparation Time: 17 minutes
Ingredients:
- 1 cup polenta
- 4 cups water
- 1 tsp salt
- 1 tbsp butter
- For roasted tomatoes:
- 2 thyme sprigs
- 2 tsp olive oil
- 2 cups grape tomatoes
- 1/2 tsp salt

Directions for Cooking:
1. Add polenta, water, butter, and salt into the instant pot and stir well.
2. Seal pot with lid and cook on porridge mode for 7 minutes.
3. Allow to release pressure naturally then open the lid.
4. Toss together Grape tomatoes, olive oil, thyme, and salt and place on baking sheet and broil for 10 minutes.
5. Mix together polenta and tomatoes.
6. Serve warm and enjoy.

Nutrition information per serving:

Calories: 200; Carbohydrates: 33.9g; Protein: 3.7g; Fat: 5.7g; Sugar: 2.8g; Sodium: 906mg

Simple Pearl Barley

Serves: 4
Preparation Time: 25 minutes
Ingredients:
- 1 1/2 cups pearl barley, rinsed and drained
- 3 cups vegetable stock
- 1 tsp salt

Directions for Cooking:
1. Add all ingredients into the instant pot and stir well.
2. Seal pot with lid and cook on manual high pressure for 25 minutes.
3. Allow to release pressure naturally then open the lid.
4. Stir and serve.

Nutrition information per serving:

Calories: 272; Carbohydrates: 59.8g; Protein: 7.4g; Fat: 2.4g; Sugar: 2.1g; Sodium: 1128mg

Lemon Dill Couscous
SmartPoints: 5
Serves: 6
Preparation Time: 7 minutes
Ingredients:
- 1 cup couscous
- 1 tbsp olive oil
- 1 tsp dried dill
- 2 cups vegetable stock
- 8 oz snap peas, trimmed
- 1 fresh lemon juice
- 1/4 tsp pepper
- 1/2 tsp salt

Directions for Cooking:
1. Add olive oil into the instant pot and set the pot on sauté mode.
2. Add couscous into the pot and stir for 1 minute. Pour broth into the pot and stir well.
3. Seal pot with lid and cook on high pressure for 5 minutes.
4. Release pressure using quick release method than open the lid.
5. Stir in snap peas, pepper, and salt. Stir well.
6. Again seal pot with lid and cook on high pressure for 1 minute.
7. Release pressure using quick release method.
8. Add lemon juice and stir well.
9. Serve and enjoy.

Nutrition information per serving:

Calories: 165; Carbohydrates: 28.8g; Protein: 5.8g; Fat: 3.4g; Sugar: 3g; Sodium: 441mg

Butter Brown Rice
SmartPoints: 5
Serves: 6
Preparation Time: 23 minutes
Ingredients:

- 2 cups brown rice
- 1 1/4 cups vegetable stock
- 1/2 cup butter
- 1 1/4 cups onion soup

Directions for Cooking:
1. Add all ingredients in instant pot mix well.
2. Seal pot with lid and select manual high pressure for 23 minutes.
3. Allow to release pressure naturally then open the lid.
4. Serve and enjoy.

Nutrition information per serving:

Calories: 391; Carbohydrates: 52.1g; Protein: 6.5g; Fat: 18.2g; Sugar: 1.8g; Sodium: 702mg

Vegetable Pesto Quinoa
SmartPoints: 5
Serves: 6
Preparation Time: 15 minutes
Ingredients:
- 1 ½ cups quinoa
- ¼ cup sliced almonds
- ½ cup feta cheese, crumbled
- 1/3 cup pesto
- ½ cup can olives
- 2 tomato, chopped
- 1 ½ cups vegetable stock
- 4 cups spinach
- 1 bell pepper, chopped
- 3 celery stalk, chopped
- ¼ tsp salt

Directions for Cooking:
1. Add all ingredients except tomatoes, pesto, olives, sliced almonds, and feta cheese into the instant pot and stir well.
2. Seal pot with lid and select manual high pressure for 1 minute.
3. Allow to release pressure naturally for 10 minutes then release using quick release method.
4. Fluff the quinoa with a fork.
5. Add pesto, olives, and tomatoes. Stir well.
6. Top with sliced almonds and feta cheese.
7. Serve and enjoy.

Nutrition information per serving:

Calories: 303; Carbohydrates: 33.8g; Protein: 11.1g; Fat: 14.7g; Sugar: 3.6g; Sodium: 565mg

Garlic Lima Beans
SmartPoints: 6
Serves: 6
Preparation Time: 50 minutes
Ingredients:
- 1 lb dry baby lima beans
- 1 bay leaf
- 1 tsp black pepper
- 4 cups water
- 3 cups vegetable stock
- 1 tbsp garlic, minced

- 1 onion, chopped
- 4 cups cooked ham, shredded

Directions for Cooking:
1. Add all ingredients into the instant pot and stir well.
2. Seal pot with lid and cook on high pressure for 25 minutes.
3. Allow to release pressure naturally for 10 minutes then release using quick release method.
4. Remove bay leaf from beans.
5. Stir well and serve.

Nutrition information per serving:

Calories: 247; Carbohydrates: 22.1g; Protein: 20.4g; Fat: 9.4g; Sugar: 2.9g; Sodium: 1546mg

Hearty White Beans with Tomato
SmartPoints:6
Serves: 6
Preparation Time: 40 minutes
Ingredients:
- 2 cups vegetable broth
- 1 tbsp olive oil
- 6 oz tomato paste
- 28 oz can plum tomatoes
- 2 ¼ cups dry cannellini beans
- 1 bay leaf
- 2 garlic cloves, minced
- 1 onion, chopped
- 4 bacon slices, cooked and chopped
- ½ tsp kosher salt

Directions for Cooking:
1. Add olive oil into the instant pot and set the pot on sauté mode.
2. Add garlic and onion to the pot and sauté until softened.
3. Add broth, tomato paste, tomatoes, beans, bay leaf, bacon, and salt. Stir well.
4. Seal pot with lid and cook on high pressure for 40 minutes.
5. Allow to release pressure naturally then open the lid.
6. Mash the tomatoes lightly with a fork. Season with pepper and salt.
7. Serve and enjoy.

Nutrition information per serving:

Calories: 390; Carbohydrates: 53.5g; Protein: 26.2g; Fat: 8.8g; Sugar: 9.2g; Sodium: 1157mg

Garlic Garbanzo Beans
SmartPoints:5
Serves: 6
Preparation Time: 35 minutes
Ingredients:
- 1 cup dry garbanzo beans, rinsed and drained
- ½ tsp chicken bouillon
- 2 bay leaves
- 4 garlic cloves
- 4 cups water

Directions for Cooking:
1. Add all ingredients into the instant pot and stir well.
2. Seal pot with lid and cook on high pressure for 35 minutes.

3. Allow to release pressure naturally for 15 minutes then release using quick release method.
4. Drain beans and serve.

Nutrition information per serving:

Calories: 124; Carbohydrates: 20.9g; Protein: 6.6g; Fat: 2g; Sugar: 3.6g; Sodium: 15mg

Classic Wild Rice
SmartPoints: 5
Serves: 6
Preparation Time: 35 minutes
Ingredients:
- 2 cups wild rice
- 5 cups chicken broth
- 2 tsp salt

Directions for Cooking:
1. Add all ingredients into the instant pot and stir well.
2. Seal pot with lid and cook on high pressure for 35 minutes.
3. Release pressure using quick release method than open the lid carefully.
4. Fluff rice with a fork and serve.

Nutrition information per serving:

Calories: 222; Carbohydrates: 40.7g; Protein: 11.9g; Fat: 1.7g; Sugar: 1.9g; Sodium: 1415mg

Vegetables

Crockpot Pumpkin Chili
SmartPoints:5
Serves: 4
Preparation Time: 2 minutes
Cooking Time: 10 minutes

Ingredients
- 3 cups pumpkin, chopped into small pieces
- 3 cups diced tomatoes
- 1 tablespoon chili powder
- 1 tablespoon nutritional yeasts
- 1 can white beans, drained and rinsed
- 1 teaspoon cumin
- Salt and pepper to taste

Directions
1. Place all ingredients in the Instant Pot.
2. Stir the contents and close the lid.
3. Close the lid and press the Manual button.
4. Adjust the cooking time to 10 minutes.
5. Do quick pressure release.
6. Serve with sour cream and avocado slices if desired.

Nutrition value:
Calories per serving: 120; Carbohydrates: 9.5g; Protein:5.2 g; Fat: 3.2g; Fiber: 7.3g

Vegan Pulled "Pork"

SmartPoints:7
Serves: 6
Preparation Time: 2 minutes
Cooking Time: 25 minutes

Ingredients
- 2 tablespoon olive oil
- ¼ cup chopped onions
- 3 cloves of garlic, minced
- 3 cans green jackfruit, packed in water and drained
- 2 cups barbecue sauce
- 1 teaspoon liquid smoke
- 1 tablespoon Spanish paprika
- 3 tablespoons nutritional yeast
- Salt and pepper

Directions
1. Press the Sauté button on the Instant Pot and heat oil.
2. Sauté the onions and garlic until fragrant.
3. Add the rest of the ingredients.
4. Close the lid and press the Manual button.
5. Adjust the cooking time to 25 minutes.
6. Do quick pressure release.

Nutrition value:
Calories per serving:207; Carbohydrates: 39g; Protein: 45g; Fat: 8g; Fiber: 32g

Instant Pot Cajun Peanuts

SmartPoints:6
Serves: 6
Preparation Time: 2 minutes
Cooking Time: 10 minutes

Ingredients
- 5 pounds raw peanuts, in shells
- 1 package dry crab boil
- 1 can jalapeno peppers
- 3 tablespoon Cajun seasoning
- 5 cups water

Directions
1. Place all ingredients in the Instant Pot.
2. Stir the contents and close the lid.
3. Close the lid and press the Manual button.
4. Adjust the cooking time to 4 minutes.
5. Do quick pressure release.
6. Drain the peanuts before serving.

Nutrition value:
Calories per serving:403; Carbohydrates:19 g; Protein: 18.6g; Fat: 37.6g; Fiber: 7g

Indian Coconut Kale Curry

SmartPoints:6
Serves: 4

Preparation Time: 2 minutes
Cooking Time: 4 minutes

Ingredients
- ¼ cup curry powder
- 1 can unsweetened coconut cream
- 1 package dry onion soup mix
- 2 cups kale, rinsed and shredded
- 1 large yellow bell pepper, cut into strips
- 1 cup cilantro for garnish

Directions
1. Place all ingredients in the Instant Pot.
2. Stir the contents and close the lid.
3. Close the lid and press the Manual button.
4. Adjust the cooking time to 4 minutes.
5. Do quick pressure release.
6. Once the lid is open, garnish with cilantro.

Nutrition value:
Calories per serving: 433; Carbohydrates: 15g; Protein: 10g; Fat: 42.7g; Fiber: 6.7g

Veggie Cheese Soup

SmartPoints:6
Serves: 6
Preparation Time: 2 minutes
Cooking Time: 7 minutes

Ingredients
- 1 package frozen vegetables
- 1 can cream of mushroom soup
- 1 jar cheese sauce
- Salt and pepper to taste
- Mozzarella cheese, shredded

Directions
1. Place the vegetables in the Instant Pot.
2. Pour the cream of mushroom soup and cheese sauce.
3. Season with salt and pepper. Stir well.
4. Sprinkle mozzarella cheese on top.
5. Close the lid and press the Manual button.
6. Adjust the cooking time to 7 minutes.
7. Do natural pressure release.

Nutrition value:
Calories per serving:196; Carbohydrates: 24.8g; Protein: 9.9g; Fat:6.6 g; Fiber: 5.7g

Instant Pot Zucchini Casserole

SmartPoints:3
Serves: 4
Preparation Time: 2 minutes
Cooking Time: 6 minutes

Ingredients
- 2 zucchinis, sliced

- 1 large onions, chopped
- 4 stalks celery, chopped
- 1 package of your favorite seasoning
- ½ cup vegetable stock
- 4 eggs, beaten
- Salt and pepper

Directions
1. Place all ingredients in the Instant Pot.
2. Stir the contents and close the lid.
3. Close the lid and press the Manual button.
4. Adjust the cooking time to 4 minutes.
5. Do natural pressure release.

Nutrition value:
Calories per serving:256; Carbohydrates:14.2 g; Protein: 5.7g; Fat: 2.4g; Fiber: 1.8g

Creamy Artichoke, Garlic, And Zucchini
SmartPoints:5
Serves: 12
Preparation Time: 2 minutes
Cooking Time: 10 minutes

Ingredients
- 2 tablespoons coconut oil
- 1 bulb garlic, minced
- 1 large artichoke hearts, cleaned and sliced
- 2 medium zucchinis, sliced
- ½ cup whipping cream
- ½ cup vegetable broth
- Salt and pepper

Directions
1. Press the Sauté button and heat the oil
2. Sauté the garlic until fragrant.
3. Add the rest of the ingredients.
4. Stir the contents and close the lid.
5. Close the lid and press the Manual button.
6. Adjust the cooking time to 10 minutes.
7. Do quick pressure release.

Nutrition value:
Calories per serving:33; Carbohydrates: 1.79g; Protein:0.57 g; Fat: 2.85g; Fiber: 0.74g

Crockpot Summer Veggies Side Dish
SmartPoints:4
Serves: 6
Preparation Time: 2 minutes
Cooking Time: 7 minutes

Ingredients
- 2 cups okra, sliced
- 1 cup grape tomatoes
- 1 cup mushroom, sliced
- 1 ½ cups onion, sliced

- 2 cups bell pepper, sliced
- 2 ½ cups zucchini, sliced
- 2 tablespoons basil, chopped
- 1 tablespoon thyme, chopped
- ½ cups balsamic vinegar
- ½ cups olive oil
- Salt and pepper

Directions
1. Place all ingredients in the Instant Pot.
2. Stir the contents and close the lid.
3. Close the lid and press the Manual button.
4. Adjust the cooking time to 7 minutes.
5. Do quick pressure release.

Nutrition value:
Calories per serving:233; Carbohydrates: 7g; Protein: 3g; Fat: 18g; Fiber:4 g

Instant Pot Basic Steamed Vegetables
SmartPoints:3
Serves: 4
Preparation Time: 2 minutes
Cooking Time: 7 minutes

Ingredients
- 2 bell peppers, cut into large slices
- 3 small zucchinis, cut into thick slices
- ½ cup peeled garlic, minced
- 1 tablespoon Italian herb mix
- 2 tablespoon olive oil

Directions
1. Place all ingredients in a mixing bowl.
2. Season with salt if desired and toss to coat everything.
3. Place a trivet in the Instant Pot and pour 1 cup of water.
4. Place the vegetables on the steamer.
5. Close the lid and press the Steam button.
6. Adjust the cooking time to 7 minutes.
7. Do quick pressure release.

Nutrition value:
Calories per serving:96; Carbohydrates: 8.01g; Protein: 1.75g; Fat: 6.91g; Fiber: 5.3g

Instant Pot French Onion Soup
SmartPoints:5
Serves: 4
Cooking Time: 2 minutes
Preparation Time: 20 minutes

Ingredients
- 6 tablespoon unsalted butter
- 3 pounds onions, chopped
- Salt and pepper to taste
- 3 cups chicken stock
- 1 bay leaf

- 2 sprigs of thyme
- 1 teaspoon fish sauce
- 1 teaspoon apple cider vinegar
- ½ cup dry sherry
- 1 pound cheese, grated
- 1 tablespoon chives for garnish
- 8 slices of bread, toasted

Directions
1. Press the Sauté button on the Instant Pot.
2. Heat the butter and sauté the onion for 10 minutes until caramelized. Stir constantly.
3. Season with salt and pepper and stir in the rest of the ingredients except for the bread.
4. Stir to combine everything.
5. Place the slices of bread on top.
6. Close the lid and press the Manual button.
7. Adjust the cooking time to 10 minutes.
8. Do natural pressure release.

Nutrition value:
Calories per serving: 749; Carbohydrates:70.1g; Protein: 30.01g; Fat:45.18g; Fiber: 5.3g

Steamed Vegetables Side Dish

SmartPoints:3
Serves: 6
Preparation Time: 2 minutes
Cooking Time:10 minutes

Ingredients
- 2 bell peppers, sliced
- 2 large zucchinis, sliced
- ½ cup peeled garlic cloves
- Salt and pepper to taste
- 1 teaspoon Italian seasoning
- 2 tablespoon olive oil
- ¼ cup parmesan cheese, grated

Directions
1. Place a trivet or steamer in the Instant Pot and pour a cup of water.
2. In a baking dish that will fit inside the Instant Pot, mix the pepper, zucchini, and garlic. Season with salt, pepper, and Italian seasoning.
3. Pour in olive oil and toss to combine.
4. Add the parmesan cheese on top.
5. Place on top of the steamer basket.
6. Close the lid and press the Steam button.
7. Adjust the cooking time to 10 minutes.
8. Do quick pressure release.

Nutrition value:
Calories per serving: 127; Carbohydrates:8.6 g; Protein: 2g; Fat: 15.3g; Fiber: 6.1g

Hummus Under Pressure

Preparation Time:minutes
SmartPoints:8
Serves: 8
Nutrition Value: Calories 161; Carbs 20g; Fat 6g; Protein 8g

Ingredients
1 Onion, quartered
1 Bay Leaf
2 tbsp Soy Sauce
¼ cup Tahini
¾ cup Garbanzo Beans
¼ cup dried Soybeans
¼ cup chopped Parsley
1 cup Vegetable Broth
Juice of 1 Lemon
2 Garlic Cloves, minced

Directions
Add garbanzo beans, soybeans, and broth in your pressure cooker. Pour some water over to cover them by one inch. Seal the lid, press SOUP/BROTH, for 20 minutes at High pressure.
When ready, release the pressure naturally for 10 minutes. Drain the beans and save the cooking liquid. Place the beans along with the remaining ingredients into a food processor.
Process until smooth. Add some of the cooking liquid to make hummus thinner, if desired.

Big Potatoes and Peas Bowl
Preparation Time:20 minutes
SmartPoints:8
Serves: 2
Nutrition Value: Calories 185; Carbs 24g; Fat 8g; Protein 8g

Ingredients
3 Sweet Potatoes, diced
1 Onion, chopped
1 cup Green Peas, fresh
2 cups Spinach, chopped
2 tsp Garlic
1 tbsp Tomato Paste
1 tbsp Oil
½ tsp Coriander
1 tsp Cumin
1 ½ cups Water

Directions
Heat oil on SAUTÉ mode at High. Cook the onions and garlic for 2 minutes, until soft and fragrant. Stir in the tomato paste and spices. Pour in the water and tomato paste. Stir to combine.
Add sweet potatoes and seal the lid. Cook for 14 minutes on PRESSURE COOK/MANUAL at High. When done, do a quick pressure release. Stir in spinach and cook until wilted, for a few minutes, on SAUTÉ, lid off.

Collard Greens Refined Hummus
Preparation Time:25 minutes
SmartPoints:6
Serves: 12
Nutrition Value: Calories 169; Carbs 22g; Fat 6g; Protein 7g

Ingredients
3 tbsp Tahini
¼ tsp ground Black Pepper
½ tsp Sea Salt
2 cups Chickpeas
1 cup Green Garlic, minced
4 ½ cups Water
2 tbsp Olive Oil
2 cups packed Collard Greens, chopped

Directions
Pour water in the pressure cooker and add the chickpeas. Seal the lid and adjust the cooking time to 20 minutes on PRESSURE COOK/MANUAL mode. Do a quick release, and drain the chickpeas.

Transfer to a food processor with the greens, garlic, salt, pepper, and tahini. Pulse until you obtain a creamy mixture. Pour gradually the oil while machine is running, until everything is well incorporated.

Saucy BBQ Veggie Meal

Preparation Time:20 minutes
SmartPoints:7
Serves: 4
Nutrition Value: Calories 244; Carbs 29g; Fat 9g; Protein 15g
Ingredients
2 Tomatoes, chopped
2 Carrots, chopped
1 cup Peas
2 Onions, chopped
1 cup Parsnips, chopped
2 Bell Peppers, diced
2 Sweet Potatoes, diced
½ cup BBQ Sauce
1 tbsp Oil
1 tbsp Ketchup
¼ tsp Cayenne Pepper
½ tsp Salt
¼ tsp Pepper
1 cup Veggie Stock
Directions
Heat oil on SAUTÉ mode at High. Add onions and cook for 2 minutes, until translucent. Add parsnips and carrots and cook for 3 more minutes, until soft. Stir in the remaining ingredients.
Seal the lid and cook for 10 minutes on PRESSURE COOK/MANUAL mode at High pressure. When ready, and do a quick pressure release. Discard the excess cooking liquid, before serving.

Vegan Swiss Chard Dip

Preparation Time:15 minutes
SmartPoints:6
Serves: 12
Nutrition Value: Calories 88; Carbs 3g; Fat 7g; Protein 3g
Ingredients
1 ½ cups Tofu
2 cups Swiss Chard, chopped
1 tsp dried Dill weed
2 tsp fresh Lemon Juice
½ tsp ground Black Pepper
1 tsp Salt
1 ¼ cups Vegan Mayonnaise
1 tsp Lemon Zest, grated for garnish
1 cup Water
Directions
Pour 1 cup water. In a baking dish, mix all ingredients, except lemon zest, and stir to combine. Cover the dish with aluminium foil. Then, make a foil sling and lower the dish on the rack.
Seal the lid, switch the pressure release valve to close and cook for 10 minutes on PRESSURE COOK/MANUAL at High Pressure. When it goes off, quick release the pressure. Sprinkle with lemon zest and serve.

Cheesy Asparagus and Spinach Dip

Preparation Time:15 minutes
SmartPoints:6
Serves: 16
Nutrition Value: Calories 118; Carbs 8g; Fat 8g; Protein 4g
Ingredients

18 oz Asparagus Spears, ends trimmed, chopped
12 ounces Spinach, thawed, drained and chopped
1 ½ cups Mozzarella Cheese, shredded
½ tsp ground Black Pepper
1 tsp Sea Salt
½ cup Mayonnaise
1 cup Heavy Cream
Directions
Insert a trivet in the pressure Cooker. Pour half cup of water. In a baking dish, add all ingredients and stir well.
Cover with aluminium foil and lower on top of the trivet. Seal the lid and cook for 12 minutes on PRESSURE COOK/MANUAL at High. Do a quick release, and serve with crackers.

Classic Easy Italian Peperonata

Preparation Time:10 minutes
SmartPoints:6
Serves: 4
Nutrition Value: Calories 152; Carbs 17g; Fat 8g; Protein 6g
Ingredients
1 Green Bell Pepper, sliced
2 Yellow Bell Peppers, sliced
2 Red Bell Peppers, sliced
3 Tomatoes, chopped
1 Red Onions, chopped
2 Garlic Cloves, minced
2 cups Veggie Stock
2 tbsp Olive Oil
Salt and Pepper, to taste
4 cup Egg Noodles, cooked optional, to serve
Directions
Heat oil on SAUTÉ mode at High, and cook the onion for 2 minutes, until translucent. Stir in peppers and stir-fry for 2 more minutes. Add garlic and cook for 1 minute, until soft.
Stir in the tomatoes and cook for 2 minutes before pouring in the stock. Seal the lid and cook for 6 minutes on STEAM mode at High. When done, do a quick pressure release.
Check the veggies whether they are soft and cooked through. If not, cook for a few more minutes, lid off, on SAUTÉ mode at High. Drain and serve over noodles.

Spicy Tomato Sauce

Preparation Time:20 minutes
SmartPoints:5
Serves: 16
Nutrition Value: Calories 50; Carbs 5g; Fat 3g; Protein 1g
Ingredients
3 pounds Tomatoes, peeled and diced
1 cup Red Onions, chopped
¼ cup Olive Oil
2 tsp Brown Sugar
½ tsp dried basil
1 Red Chilli, chopped
½ tsp dried Oregano
2 Cloves Garlic, minced
½ tsp dried Sage
Salt and ground Black Pepper, to taste
½ cup Water
Directions

1. Select SAUTÉ mode at High and heat the oil; cook the green onions and garlic until tender, for about 3 minutes. Add the remaining ingredients and seal the lid. Select PRESSURE COOK/MANUAL mode.
2. Cook for 10 minutes at High Pressure. Do a quick pressure release. Cool before serving.

Appetizers

Chives Salmon Bites

Preparation time: 10 minutes
Cooking time: 10 minutes
SmartPoints:5
Serves: 8

Ingredients:
- 1 tablespoon lemon juice
- 1 tablespoon olive oil
- 1 pound salmon fillets, boneless, skinless and cubed
- 2 garlic cloves, minced
- 1 tablespoon chives, chopped
- 1 tablespoon lime zest, grated
- 1 cup water

Directions:
In a bowl, mix the salmon cubes with the rest of the ingredients except the chives and the water and toss.
Put the water in your instant pot, add the steamer basket, add the salmon inside, put the lid on and cook on High for 10 minutes.
Release the pressure naturally for 10 minutes, arrange the salmon biter on a platter, sprinkle the chives on top and serve.

Nutrition Value: calories 180, fat 3, fiber 3, carbs 7, protein 9

Eggplant Salad

Preparation time: 5 minutes
Cooking time: 10 minutes
SmartPoints:3
Serves: 4

Ingredients:
- 2 eggplants, roughly cubed
- Zest and juice of 2 limes
- 2 teaspoons cumin, ground
- 2 tablespoons olive oil
- 1 cup tomato, cubed
- ½ cup spring onions, chopped
- 2 tablespoons garlic, minced
- 1 Serrano chili pepper, chopped
- ¼ cup cilantro, chopped

Directions:
Set the instant pot on Sauté mode, add the oil, heat it up, add the onions, garlic and chili pepper and sauté for 2 minutes.
Add the rest of the ingredients, put the lid on and cook on High for 8 minutes.
Release the pressure fast for 5 minutes, divide the salad into cups and serve as an appetizer.

Nutrition Value: calories 150, fat 9, fiber 2, carbs 6, protein 6

Basil Shrimp Salad

Preparation time: 5 minutes
Cooking time: 6 minutes
SmartPoints:6
Serves: 4

Ingredients:
- ½ cup lime juice
- 1 red onion, chopped
- ½ teaspoon hot sauce
- ½ cup balsamic vinegar
- 1 and ½ pounds shrimp, peeled and deveined
- 1 tablespoon olive oil
- 2 tablespoons basil, chopped

Directions:
Set the instant pot on Sauté mode, add the oil, heat it up, add the onion and sauté for 2 minutes.
Add the rest of the ingredients, put the lid on and cook on High for 4 minutes.
Release the pressure fast for 5 minutes, divide the shrimp mix into small bowls and serve.

Nutrition Value: calories 173, fat 9, fiber 3, carbs 5, protein 8

Spinach Dip

Preparation time: 5 minutes
Cooking time: 8 minutes
SmartPoints:6
Serves: 4

Ingredients:
- 15 ounces spinach leaves
- 2 tablespoons coconut cream
- A pinch of salt and black pepper
- 2 tablespoons olive oil
- 4 garlic cloves, roasted and minced
- 2 tablespoons lemon juice

Directions:
In your instant pot, combine all the ingredients except the cream, put the lid on and cook on Low for 8 minutes.
Release the pressure fast for 5 minutes, add the cream, blend the mix using an immersion blender, divide into bowls and serve.

Nutrition Value: calories 183, fat 9, fiber 4, carbs 7, protein 5

Mint Spinach and Shrimp Salad

Preparation time: 5 minutes
Cooking time: 10 minutes
SmartPoints:6
Serves: 4

Ingredients:
- 1 pound spinach leaves, torn
- 1 pound shrimp, peeled and deveined
- 1 shallot, sliced
- ½ tablespoons olive oil
- 2 tablespoons mint leaves, chopped
- ½ cup coconut cream
- A pinch of salt and black pepper

Directions:
Set the instant pot on Sauté mode, add the oil, heat it up, add the shallot and sauté for 2 minutes.
Add the rest of the ingredients, put the lid on and cook on Low for 8 minutes.
Release the pressure fast for 5 minutes, divide the mix into bowls and serve as an appetizer.

Nutrition Value: calories 180, fat 9, fiber 2, carbs 6, protein 9

Red Beans Spread

Preparation time: 10 minutes
Cooking time: 18 minutes
SmartPoints: 5
Serves: 6

Ingredients:
- 1 pound red beans, soaked overnight and drained
- 1 cup red onion, chopped
- 4 cups veggie stock
- 1 tablespoon sweet paprika
- 1 tablespoon lime juice
- 2 tablespoons olive oil
- 2 garlic cloves, minced

Directions:
In your instant pot, combine the beans with the stock, put the lid on and cook on High for 18 minutes.
Release the pressure naturally, drain the beans, transfer them to a blender, add ½ cup cooking liquid and the rest of the ingredients and pulse well.
Divide the spread into bowls and serve as an appetizer.

Nutrition Value: calories 210, fat 7, fiber 4, carbs 6, protein 10

Cod Salad

Preparation time: 10 minutes
Cooking time: 10 minutes
SmartPoints: 4
Serves: 4

Ingredients:
- 1 teaspoon avocado oil
- 1 pound cod fillets, boneless, skinless and cubed
- A pinch of salt and black pepper
- 2 tomatoes, cubed
- 1 teaspoon oregano, dried
- 1 teaspoon rosemary, dried

- 1 and ½ cups baby arugula
- 1 tablespoon lime juice
- 1 red onion, chopped

Directions:
Set the instant pot on Sauté mode, add the oil, heat it up, add the onion and sauté for 2 minutes.
Add the rest of the ingredients except the arugula, put the lid on and cook on High for 8 minutes.
Release the pressure naturally for 10 minutes, transfer the cod mix to a bowl, add the arugula, toss and serve.

Nutrition Value: calories 180, fat 9, fiber 4, carbs 6, protein 8

Pesto Shrimp and Tomato Salad

Preparation time: 10 minutes
Cooking time: 8 minutes
SmartPoints: 7
Serves: 4

Ingredients:
- 1 and ½ pounds shrimp, peeled and deveined
- 2 tablespoons parsley, chopped
- 2 tablespoons basil pesto
- 2 teaspoons lime juice
- 1 tablespoon olive oil
- A pinch of salt and black pepper
- ½ pound cherry tomatoes, cubed
- 1 cup baby arugula

Directions:
In your instant pot, combine all the ingredients except the arugula, toss, put the lid on and cook on Low for 8 minutes.
Release the pressure naturally for 10 minutes, transfer the mix to a bowl, add the arugula, toss and serve as an appetizer.

Nutrition Value: calories 177, fat 8, fiber 2, carbs 6, protein 7

Chicken and Peppers Salad

Preparation time: 10 minutes
Cooking time: 15 minutes
SmartPoints: 8
Serves: 4

Ingredients:
- 1 pound chicken breast, skinless, boneless and cubed
- 1 pound mixed bell peppers, cut into strips
- 2 tablespoons olive oil
- 2 cups red onion, chopped
- 2 tablespoons garlic, chopped
- 1 cup chicken stock
- 1 cup tomatoes, crushed
- 1 tablespoon basil, chopped

Directions:

Set your instant pot on Sauté mode, add the oil, heat it up, add the chicken and the onion and brown for 5 minutes.
Add the rest of the ingredients except the basil, put the lid on and cook on High for 10 minutes.
Release the pressure naturally for 10 minutes, divide the mix into bowls, sprinkle the basil on top and serve as an appetizer.

Nutrition Value: calories 221, fat 12, fiber 4, carbs 7, protein 11

Mussels and Spinach Bowls

Preparation time: 10 minutes
Cooking time: 10 minutes
SmartPoints:7
Serves: 4

Ingredients:
- 2 pounds mussels, cleaned and scrubbed
- 1 red onion, chopped
- 1 pound baby spinach
- ½ cup chicken stock
- 2 garlic cloves, minced
- 1 teaspoon chili powder
- 1 tablespoon chives, chopped
- 1 tablespoon olive oil

Directions:
Set instant pot on Sauté mode, add the oil, heat it up, add the onion and the garlic, stir and sauté for 2 minutes.
Add the rest of the ingredients except the spinach and the chives, put the lid on and cook on Low for 8 minutes.
Release the pressure naturally for 10 minutes, transfer the mussels mix to a bowl, add the spinach and the chives and toss.
Divide the salad into small bowls and serve as an appetizer.

Nutrition Value: calories 180, fat 9, fiber 3, carbs 5, protein 7

Tomato Salsa

Preparation time: 5 minutes
Cooking time: 7 minutes
SmartPoints:7
Serves: 4

Ingredients:
- 1 and ½ pound cherry tomatoes, cubed
- 2 chili peppers, chopped
- ¼ cup veggie stock
- 2 tablespoons olive oil
- ¼ cup balsamic vinegar
- 2 red onions, chopped
- 1 tablespoon basil, chopped
- 1 tablespoon parsley, chopped
- 1 tablespoon chives, chopped
- 1 cucumber, cubed

Directions:
In your instant pot, combine the tomatoes with the chili peppers and stock, put the lid on and cook on Low for 7 minutes.
Release the pressure fast for 5 minutes, transfer the tomatoes to a bowl, add the rest of the ingredients, toss, divide into cups and serve.

Nutrition Value: calories 140, fat 4, fiber 3, carbs 5, protein 4

Hot Mussels Salad

Preparation time: 6 minutes
Cooking time: 10 minutes
SmartPoints: 6
Serves: 4

Ingredients:
- 2 pounds mussels, scrubbed
- 1 and ½ cups baby spinach
- 2 tablespoons olive oil
- 1 yellow onion, chopped
- 1 teaspoon hot paprika
- 14 ounces tomatoes, chopped
- 2 teaspoons garlic, minced
- 2 teaspoons oregano, dried
- 1 teaspoon basil, dried
- 1 tablespoon parsley, chopped

Directions:
Set your instant pot on Sauté mode, add the oil, heat it up, add the onion and the garlic and sauté for 2 minutes.
Add the rest of the ingredients except the parsley, put the lid on and cook on Low for 7 minutes.
Release the pressure fast for 6 minutes, divide the mussels mix into small bowls, sprinkle the parsley on top and serve.

Nutrition Value: calories 176, fat 4, fiber 3, carbs 6, protein 7

Turkey Salad

Preparation time: 10 minutes
Cooking time: 15 minutes
SmartPoints: 7
Serves: 4

Ingredients:
- 1 and ½ pounds turkey breast, skinless, boneless and cubed
- 2 tomatoes, cubed
- 2 red bell peppers, cut into strips
- 1 tablespoon olive oil
- 2 red onions, chopped
- ½ cup parsley, chopped
- 20 ounces canned tomatoes, chopped
- 1 tablespoon basil, chopped
- A pinch of salt and black pepper

- 1 cup baby arugula
- ½ cup baby spinach

Directions:
1. Set your instant pot on Sauté mode, add the oil, heat it up, add the onions and the turkey and sauté for 5 minutes.
2. Add the rest of the ingredients except the basil, arugula and spinach, put the lid on and cook on High for 10 minutes.
3. Release the pressure naturally for 10 minutes, transfer the mix to a bowl, add the arugula, basil and spinach and toss.
4. Divide between plates and serve as an appetizer right away.

Nutrition Value: calories 181, fat 4, fiber 3, carbs 7, protein 15

Silician Meat Sauce

Preparation time: 10 minutes
Cook time: 35 minutes

SmartPoints: 4
Serves: 12
Ingredients:
- 3 tbsp. of olive oil, divided
- 2 lbs. of boneless country-style pork ribs
- 1 medium onion, chopped
- 3 to 5 garlic cloves, minced
- 2 cans (28 oz. each crushed or diced tomatoes
- 1 can (6 oz. Italian tomato paste
- 3 bay leaves
- 2 tbsp. of chopped fresh parsley
- 2 tbsp. of chopped capers, drained
- ½ tsp. of dried basil
- ½ tsp. of dried rosemary, crushed
- ½ tsp. of dried thyme
- ½ tsp. of crushed red pepper flakes
- ½ tsp. of salt
- ½ tsp. of sugar
- 1 cup of beef broth
- ½ cup of dry red wine or additional beef broth
- Hot cooked pasta
- Grated Parmesan cheese, optional

Directions:
1. Press the Sauté function on a 6-qt. electric pressure cooker. Adjust for high heat and add 2 tablespoons of olive oil.
2. Brown the pork on each side in batches and set aside. Add the rest of the oil and sauté the onion for about 2 minutes.
3. Add the garlic and cook for additional 1 minute. Add the next 11 ingredients. Place the meat your pressure cooker. Add in broth and red wine. Bring the pot to a boil.
4. Close and lock the lid in place and ensure that the valve is in sealing position. Select Manual function to cook on High Pressure for about 35 minutes.
5. When the time is up, use a natural pressure release for about 10 minutes, then quick release any remaining pressure.
6. Carefully open the lid and remove the bay leaves. Remove the meat from pressure cooker and shred, discarding bones. Add the meat to the sauce and give everything a good stir.
7. Serve over pasta; if desired, sprinkle with Parmesan cheese.

Cranberry Pecan Brie

Preparation time: 15 minutes

Cooking time: 30 minutes

SmartPoints: 4

Serves: 4

Ingredients:
- 1 (8-oz round of Brie
- ¼ cup of cranberry jalapeno preSmartPoints: Serves
- 3 tbsp. candied pecans
- 1 tsp. minced fresh thyme

Directions:
1. Slice through the rind on top of the Brie in a grid pattern.
2. Add the Brie in a baking dish in a way it will fit in your instant pot and then cover baking dish tightly with foil.
3. Prepare a foil sling for lifting the baking dish out of the Instant Pot by taking an 18" strip of foil and folding it twice.
4. Add 1 cup of water into the Instant Pot and place the rack in the bottom. Keep the baking dish on center of the foil strip.
5. Lower it into the instant pot on to the rack. Fold the foil strips down so they may not disturb you when closing the lid.
6. Close and lock the lid in place and ensure that the valve is in sealing position. Press the manual setting to cook on high pressure for about 20 minutes.
7. When the time is up, use a natural pressure release for about 10 minutes. You can now inspect to make sure cheese is melted and piping hot.
8. Scoop to a serving plate and top with preSmartPoints: Serves, pecans and thyme.
9. Serve immediately and enjoy!

Tavern Burgers

Preparation time: 5 minutes

Cook time: 15 minutes

SmartPoints:12

Serves: 8

Ingredients:
- 2 lbs. of ground beef
- 3 green onions, chopped
- ½ tsp. of salt
- ¼ tsp. of pepper
- 10¾ oz. can chicken gumbo soup, partially drained
- 10¾ oz. tomato soup
- 2 tbsp. of mustard
- 1 tbsp. of ketchup
- 8 slices American cheese
- Sandwich Buns, split

Directions:
1. Press the Sauté function on your Instant Pot.
2. Add the ground beef and cook until no longer pink. Push the Cancel button and drain.
3. Add the rest of the ingredients (except cheese and bun to your Instant Pot.
4. Close and lock the lid in place and ensure that the valve is in sealing position.
5. Select Manual function to cook on High Pressure for about 7 minutes.
6. When the time is up, use a quick pressure release.
7. Carefully open the lid and spoon the beef mixture onto bun and add cheese slice to serve.
8. Serve and enjoy!

Dessert

Mini Lemon Cheesecakes

Preparation Time: 5 minutes
SmartPoints: 8
Serve: 6

Ingredients:

1 tbsp lemon zest, grated
1 tsp lemon juice
½ tsp stevia powder orTruvia
1/4 cup coconut oil, softened
4 tbsp unsalted butter, softened
4 ounces cream cheeseheavy cream

Directions:

1. Blend all ingredients together with a hand mixer or blender until smooth and creamy.
2. Prepare a cupcake or muffin tin with 6 paper liners.
3. Pour mixture into prepared tin and place in freezer for 23 hours or until firm.
4. Sprinkle cups with additional lemon zest. Or try using chopped nuts or shredded, unsweetened coconut.

Nutritional Value
Calories 213
Fats 23g
Carbohydrates: 0.7g
Protein 1.5g

Chocolate Layered Coconut Cups

Preparation Time: 55 minutes
SmartPoints:8
Serve: 10

Ingredients:

Bottom Layer:
1/2 cup unsweetened, shredded coconut
3 tbsp powdered sweeteners such as Splenda or Truvia
1/2 cup coconut butter
1/2 cup coconut oil
Top Layer:
1 1/2 ounces cocoa butter
1ounce unsweetened chocolate
1/4 cup cocoa powder
1/2 tsp vanilla extract
1/4 cup powdered sweetener such as Splenda or Truvia

Directions:

1. Prepare a minimuffin pan with 20 mini paper liners.

For the bottom layer:

2. Combine coconut oil and coconut butter in a small saucepan over low heat.
3. Stir until smooth and melted then add the shredded coconut and powdered sweetener until well combined.
4. Divide the mixture among prepared mini muffin cups and place in the refrigerator for 30 minutes.

For the top layer:

1. Combine cocoa butter and unsweetened chocolate together in double boiler or a bowl set over a pan of simmering water. Stir until melted.
2. Stir in the powdered sweetener, then the cocoa powder and mix until smooth.

3. Remove from heat and stir in the vanilla extract.
4. Spoon chocolate mixture over coconut candies and let them set for 15 minutes.
5. Serve and enjoy.

Nutritional Value
Calories 300
Fats 27g
Carbohydrates: 14.5g
Protein 2g

Pumpkin Pie Chocolate Cups

Preparation Time: 45 minutes
Serve: 18

Ingredients:

For the crust:
ounces extra dark chocolate 85% cocoa solids or more
2 tbsp coconut oil
For the pie:
½ cup coconut butter
¼ cup coconut oil
2 tsp pumpkin pie spice mix
½ cup unsweetened pumpkin puree
2 tbsp healthy lowcarb sweetener
Optional: 1520 drops liquid stevia for added sweetness

Directions:

1. Place the chocolate and coconut oil in a double boiler or a glass bowl on top of a small saucepan filled with simmering water. Once completely melted, remove from the heat and set aside.
2. Prepare a mini muffin tin with 18 paper liners.
3. Fill each of the 18 mini muffin cups with 2 tsp of the chocolate mixture.
4. Place the chocolate in the refrigerator for 10 minutes.
5. Place the coconut butter, coconut oil, sweetener and pumpkin spice mix into a bowl and melt just like you did the chocolate.
6. Add the pumpkin puree and mix until smooth and well combined.
7. Remove the muffin cups from the fridge and add a heaping tsp of the pumpkin & coconut mixture into every cup.
8. Place back in the refrigerator and let it sit for 30 minutes.
9. When done, keep refrigerated. Coconut oil and butter get very soft at room temperature.
10. *Store in the refrigerator.*
11. *Serve and enjoy.*

Nutritional Value
Calories 92
Fats 9.1g
Carbohydrates: 3.4g
Protein 0.7g

Fudgy Cake

Preparation Time: 3 HR 20 minutes

Serve: 10

Ingredients:

1 1/2 cups coconut flour
1/4 cup wheyProtein powderchocolate, vanilla, and unflavored all work fine
3/4 cup sugar substitute such as Swerve or Truvia
2/3 cup cocoa powder
2 tsp baking powder

1/4 tsp salt
1/2 cup butter, melted
4 large eggs
3/4 cup almond, unsweetened
1 tsp vanilla essence
1/2 cup chopped dark chocolate, 85% cocoa or higher
Whipped cream toppingoptional:
1/2 cup heavy whipping cream
2 tbsp sugar substitute

Directions:
1. Grease the insert of a 6quart slow cooker well with butter or coconut oil.
2. In a medium bowl, whisk together almond flour, sugar substitute, cocoa powder, wheyProtein powder, baking powder, and salt.
3. Stir in butter, eggs, almond milk and vanilla extract until well combined, then fold in the chopped dark chocolate.
4. Pour into the greased slow cooker and cook on low for 2.5 to 3 hours. It will be gooey and like a pudding cake at 2.5 hours and little more cakelike at 3 hours.
5. Turn slow cooker off and let cool for 20 to 30 minutes. Cut into pieces and serve warm.
6. Best when served with freshly whipped cream. To make this, mix the whipping cream and sugar substitute together with your stand mixer, or a hand mixer. Continue mixing until soft peaks form.

Nutritional Value

Calories 313
Fats 26g
Carbohydrates: 14g
Protein 10g

196. Strawberry Cheesecake Ice Cream Cups

Preparation Time: 10 minutes
Serve: 12

Ingredients:

1/2 strawberries, fresh or frozen, mashed well
3/4 cup cream cheese, softened
1/4 cup coconut oil, softened
1015 drops liquid stevia
1 tsp vanilla extract

Directions:
1. Combine all ingredients in a mediumsized bowl and mix with a hand mixer until smooth and creamy. Can also be done in a food processor or highspeed blender.
2. Spoon the mixture into mini muffin silicon molds or small candy molds. Place in the freezer for about 2 hours or until set.
3. When done, unmold the fat bombs and place into a container. Keep in the freezer and enjoy anytime!

Nutritional Value

Calories 91
Fats 9.6g
Carbohydrates: 0.5g
Protein 1.1g

Peppermint Patties

Preparation Time: 10 minutes

Serve: 12

Ingredients:

¾ cup melted coconut butter
¼ cup finely shredded, unsweetened coconut
2 tbsp cacao powder
3 tbsp coconut oil, melted
½ tsp pure peppermint extract

Directions:

1. Mix together melted coconut butter, shredded coconut, 1 tbsp of coconut oil and peppermint extract
2. Pour coconut butter mixture into mini muffin tins that have been lined with paper liners. Fill halfway.
3. Place in refrigerator and allow to harden for about 15 minutes.
4. Mix together 2 tbsp coconut oil and cacao powder.
5. Remove muffin tin from the refrigerator and top each one with chocolate mixture.
6. Return to refrigerator until the chocolate has set.
7. When ready to eat, simply set the peppermint patty cups on the counter for about 5 minutes and unmold from muffin tin.

Nutritional Value
Calories 137
Fats 22.6g
Carbohydrates: 4.4g
Protein 1.3g

Buttery Pecan Delights

Preparation Time: 15 minutes

Serve: 2

Ingredients:

8 pecan halves
1 tbsp unsalted butter, softened
2 ounces Neufchatel cheese
1 tsp orange zest, finely grated
Pinch of sea salt

Directions:

1. Toast the pecans at 350 degrees F for 510 minutes, check often to prevent burning.
2. Mix the butter, Neufchatel cheese, and orange zest until smooth and creamy.
3. Spread the butter mixture between the cooled pecan halves and sandwich together.
4. Sprinkle with sea salt and enjoy.

Nutritional Value
Calories 129
Fats 12.8g
Carbohydrates: 1.2g
Protein 3g

Squash and Carrots Pudding

Preparation time: 10 minutes
Cooking time: 25 minutes
Serves: 4

Ingredients:
- 1 butternut squash, peeled and grated
- 2 eggs, whisked
- 2 cups water
- 1 cup almond milk
- ¾ cup coconut sugar
- 2 carrots, peeled and grated
- 1 teaspoon cinnamon powder
- Cooking spray

Directions:
In a bowl, mix the squash with the eggs and the rest of the ingredients except the water and the cooking spray and whisk well.
Grease a pudding pan with the cooking spray and pour the squash and carrots mix inside.
Add the water to the instant pot, add the steamer basket, put the pudding pan inside, put the lid on and cook on High for 25 minutes.
Release the pressure naturally for 10 minutes, cool the pudding down and serve.

Nutrition Value: calories 200, fat 5, fiber 2, carbs 5, protein 6

Tapioca and Quinoa Pudding

Preparation time: 10 minutes
Cooking time: 10 minutes

Serves: 6

Ingredients:
- 2 and ½ cups coconut milk
- 1/3 cup tapioca pearls, rinsed
- ½ cup quinoa
- ½ cup coconut sugar
- 1 teaspoon cinnamon powder

Directions:
In your instant pot, mix the coconut milk with tapioca and the rest of the ingredients, stir, put the lid on and cook on High for 10 minutes.
Release the pressure naturally for 10 minutes, divide the pudding into bowls and serve.

Nutrition Value: calories 172, fat 4, fiber 2, carbs 4, protein 5

Indian Rice Pudding

Serves: 6
Preparation Time: 35 minutes
Ingredients:
- 1 cup basmati rice, rinsed and drained
- 1 1/2 cups sugar
- 1/2 cup walnuts
- 1 cup water
- 5 cups milk

Directions for Cooking:
1. Add rice, 2 cups milk, and half sugar into the instant pot and stir well.
2. Seal pot with lid and cook on manual mode for 30 minutes
3. Meanwhile, Soak walnut into the water for 15 minutes.

4. Add walnuts and 1/2 cup water into the food processor and process until a coarse paste.
5. Release pressure using quick release method than open the lid.
6. Mash rice with a ladle.
7. Set instant pot on sauté mode. Add remaining milk, walnut paste, and sugar.
8. Stir well and simmer for 3 minutes.
9. Serve and enjoy.

Nutrition information per serving:

Calorie: 466; Carbohydrates: 85.7g; Protein: 11.4g; Fat: 10.5g; Sugar: 59.3g; Sodium: 99mg

Coconut Cake

Serves: 8
Preparation Time: 50 minutes
Ingredients:
- Dry ingredients:
- 1 tsp apple pie spice
- 1/3 cup Swerve
- 1/2 cup shredded coconut
- 1 cup almond flour
- 1 tsp baking powder
- Wet ingredients:
- 1/4 cup butter, melted
- 2 eggs, lightly beaten
- 1/2 cup heavy whipping cream

Directions for Cooking:
1. In a large bowl, mix together all dry ingredients until well combined.
2. Add all wet ingredients into the dry mixture and beat until well combined.
3. Spray 6" baking dish with cooking spray. Pour batter into the prepared baking dish.
4. Pour 2 cups water into the instant pot then place a trivet in the pot.
5. Place baking dish on top of the trivet. Seal pot with lid and cook on high pressure for 40 minutes.
6. Allow to release pressure naturally for 10 minutes then release using quick release method.
7. Remove baking dish from the pot and set aside to cool completely.
8. Serve and enjoy.

Nutrition information per serving:

Calorie: 192; Carbohydrates: 4.6g; Protein: 4.8; Fat: 18.3g; Sugar: 0.9g; Sodium: 61mg

Brown Rice Pudding

Serves: 4
Preparation Time: 35 minutes
Ingredients:
- 1 cup brown rice
- 1 tbsp butter
- 1 cinnamon stick
- 1 tbsp vanilla extract
- 1 1/2 cup water
- 1/2 cup heavy cream
- 3 tbsp honey
- 1 cup raisins

Directions for Cooking:
1. Add rice, cinnamon stick, vanilla, butter, and water into the instant pot and stir well.
2. Seal pot with lid and select manual and set timer for 20 minutes.
3. Allow to release pressure naturally for 10 minutes then release using quick release method.

4. Discard cinnamon stick from the pot.
5. Stir in cream, honey, and raisins. Set pot on sauté mode and simmer for 5 minutes.
6. Serve and enjoy.

Nutrition information per serving:

Calorie: 415; Carbohydrates: 78.7g; Protein: 5.1g; Fat: 9.9g; Sugar: 34.8g; Sodium: 36mg

Egg Custard

Serves: 6
Preparation Time: 17 minutes
Ingredients:
- 6 eggs
- 3/4 cup Swerve
- 4 cups cream
- 1 tsp vanilla

Directions for Cooking:
1. In a large mixing bowl, beat eggs. Add cream, vanilla, and swerve and blend until well combined.
2. Pour blended mixture into the baking dish and cover with foil.
3. Pour 1 1/2 cups of water into the instant pot then place a trivet in the pot.
4. Place baking dish on top of the trivet. Seal pot with lid and cook o high pressure for 7 minutes.
5. Allow to release pressure naturally for 10 minutes then release using quick release method.
6. Serve and enjoy.

Nutrition information per serving:

Calorie: 168; Carbohydrates: 5.7g; Protein: 6.8g; Fat: 13.3g; Sugar: 3.6g; Sodium: 114mg

Sweet Potato Pudding

Serves: 8
Preparation Time: 8 minutes
Ingredients:
- 1 medium sweet potato, peeled and shredded
- 1 tsp cinnamon
- 1 1/2 cups water
- 1/2 cup honey
- 12 oz milk
- 1 can coconut milk
- 2/3 cup raisins
- 1 cup Arborio rice
- 1/2 tsp cardamom
- 1 tsp vanilla
- 1 tbsp butter
- 1 tsp salt

Directions for Cooking:
1. Add butter into the instant pot and set the pot on sauté mode.
2. Add honey, water, milk, and coconut milk. Stir well.
3. Add cinnamon, vanilla, cardamom, and salt and stir well and simmer.
4. Add rice and sweet potato. Stir well.
5. Seal pot with lid and cook on high for 8 minutes.
6. Release pressure using quick release method than open the lid.
7. Stir in raisins and serve.

Nutrition information per serving:

Calorie: 251; Carbohydrates: 51.7g; Protein: 3.9g; Fat: 4g; Sugar: 27.5g; Sodium: 335mg

Coconut Custard

Serves: 4
Preparation Time: 40 minutes
Ingredients:
- 3 eggs
- 1 cup coconut milk
- 1 tsp vanilla extract
- 1/3 cup Swerve

Directions for Cooking:
1. Spray 6-inch baking dish with cooking spray and set aside.
2. In a large mixing bowl, blend together eggs, vanilla, swerve, and coconut milk.
3. Pour blended mixture into the baking dish and cover dish with foil
4. Pour 2 cups water into the instant pot than place trivet in the pot.
5. Place baking dish on top of the trivet. Seal pot with lid and cook on high for 30 minutes.
6. Allow to release pressure naturally for 10 minutes then release using quick release method.
7. Remove dish from the pot and set aside to cool completely.
8. Place in refrigerator for 3-4 hours.
9. Serve and enjoy.

Nutrition information per serving:

Calorie: 189; Carbohydrates: 3.9g; Protein: 5.5g; Fat: 17.6g; Sugar: 2.4g; Sodium: 55mg

Creamy Pecan Pudding

Serves: 8
Preparation Time: 30 minutes
Ingredients:
- 1 cup arborio rice
- 1 tbsp butter
- 1 cup brown rice
- 1 cup water
- 1 cup half and half
- 1/2 cup pecans, chopped
- 2 tsp vanilla
- 1/2 cup heavy cream
- 1 tsp salt

Directions for Cooking:
1. Add butter into the instant pot and set the pot on sauté mode.
2. Add pecans into the pot and stir until toasted.
3. Add remaining ingredients except for heavy cream and vanilla and stir well.
4. Seal pot with lid and select manual mode for 20 minutes.
5. Allow to release pressure naturally for 10 minutes then release using quick release method.
6. Stir in vanilla and heavy cream.
7. Serve and enjoy.

Nutrition information per serving:

Calories: 265; Carbohydrates: 38.9g; Protein: 4.6g; Fat: 9.7g; Sugar: 0.3g; Sodium: 320mg

Pumpkin Pudding
Servings: 6
Preparation Time: 30 minutes
Ingredients:
- 2 eggs
- 1 tsp vanilla
- 3/4 cup Swerve
- 1/2 cup heavy whipping cream
- 1 tsp pumpkin pie spice
- 15 oz can pumpkin puree

Directions for Cooking:
1. In a large mixing bowl, whisk eggs with remaining ingredients until well combined.
2. Spray 6*3 inch baking dish with cooking spray and set aside.
3. Pour batter into the prepared baking dish.
4. Pour 1 1/2 cups water into the instant pot then place a trivet in the pot.
5. Place baking dish on top of the trivet. Seal pot with lid and cook on high for 20 minutes.
6. Allow to release pressure naturally for 10 minutes then release using quick release method.
7. Remove baking dish from the instant pot and set aside to cool completely.
8. Place in refrigerator for 4-5 hours.
9. Serve and enjoy.

Nutrition information per serving:

Calories: 164; Carbohydrates: 25.9g; Protein: 4.6g; Fat: 5.2g; Sugar: 10.2g; Sodium: 37mg

Almond and Apples Bowls

Preparation time: 10 minutes
Cooking time: 20 minutes

Serves: 4

Ingredients:
- 1 cup almonds, chopped
- 2 eggs, whisked
- 1 cup coconut milk
- ¾ cup coconut sugar
- 1 teaspoon vanilla extract
- 1 cup apples, cored and cubed

Directions:
In your instant pot, mix the almonds with the eggs and the rest of the ingredients, put the lid on and cook on Low for 20 minutes.
Release the pressure naturally for 10 minutes, divide the mix into bowls and serve.

Nutrition Value: calories 172, fat 2, fiber 2, carbs 4, protein 6

Coconut Grapes Cream

Preparation time: 10 minutes
Cooking time: 15 minutes

Serves: 4

Ingredients:
- 2 cups grapes, halved

- 1 cup coconut cream
- 1 tablespoon cinnamon powder
- ½ cup coconut sugar
- 1 cup water

Directions:
In a bowl, mix the grapes with the rest of the ingredients, stir and divide into 4 ramekins.
Add the water to the instant pot, add the steamer basket, put the ramekins inside, put the lid on and cook on High for 15 minutes.
Release the pressure naturally for 10 minutes and serve the cream cold.

Nutrition Value: calories 172, fat 3, fiber 2, carbs 6, protein 6

Orange Cream

Preparation time: 10 minutes
Cooking time: 15 minutes

Serves: 4

Ingredients:
- 2 cups coconut cream
- 1 teaspoon vanilla extract
- 4 tablespoons coconut sugar
- ¼ cup orange juice
- Zest of 1 orange, grated
- 1 cup water

Directions:
In a bowl, mix the cream with the vanilla extract and the rest of the ingredients except the water, whisk well and divide into 4 ramekins.
Add the water to the instant pot, add the steamer basket, put the ramekins inside, put the lid on and cook on High for 15 minutes.
Release the pressure naturally for 10 minutes and serve right away.

Nutrition Value: calories 162, fat 2, fiber 2, carbs 4, protein 6

Egg Pudding

Preparation time: 5 minutes
Cooking time: 20 minutes

Serves: 4

Ingredients:
- 4 egg yolks, whisked
- 1 teaspoon baking powder
- 2 cups coconut cream
- ½ teaspoon vanilla extract
- 1 cup coconut sugar
- ½ cup raisins
- 1 cup water

Directions:
In a bowl mix the egg yolks with the cream and the rest of the ingredients except the water, whisk well and divide into 4 ramekins.
Add the water to the pot, add the steamer basket, add the ramekins inside, put the lid on and cook on High for 20 minutes.
Release the pressure fast for 5 minutes, and serve the pudding cold.

Nutrition Value: calories 200, fat 4, fiber 2, carbs 5, protein 4

Cinnamon Apples juice

Preparation time: 10 minutes
Cooking time: 10 minutes

Serves: 4

Ingredients:
- 4 apples, cored and cut into wedges
- 1 teaspoon vanilla extract
- 1 tablespoon cinnamon powder
- 1 cup apple juice
- ½ cup orange juice
- 2 tablespoons coconut sugar

Directions:
In your instant pot, mix the apples with the vanilla and the rest of the ingredients, put the lid on and cook on High for 10 minutes.
Release the pressure naturally for 10 minutes, divide the mix into bowls and serve.

Nutrition Value: calories 182, fat 4, fiber 2, carbs 4, protein 6

Lime Pear Bowls

Preparation time: 10 minutes
Cooking time: 10 minutes

Serves: 4

Ingredients:
- 4 pears, cored and cut into wedges
- Juice of 1 lime
- Zest of 1 lime, grated
- 1 cup apple juice
- ½ teaspoon vanilla extract

Directions:
In your instant pot, mix the pears with lime juice and the rest of the ingredients, put the lid on and cook on High for 10 minutes.
Release the pressure naturally for 10 minutes, divide the mix into bowls and serve.

Nutrition Value: calories 162, fat 2, fiber 2, carbs 4, protein 6

Apple and Cauliflower Rice Pudding

Preparation time: 10 minutes
Cooking time: 15 minutes
Serves: 4

Ingredients:
- 2 cups cauliflower rice
- 1 cup apples, cored and cubed
- 3 cups almond milk
- 3 tablespoon coconut sugar
- 1 teaspoon vanilla extract
- 1 tablespoon cinnamon powder

Directions:
In your instant pot, mix the cauliflower rice with the apples and the rest of the ingredients, put the lid on and cook on High for 15 minutes.
Release the pressure naturally for 10 minutes, divide the rice into bowls and serve.

Nutrition Value: calories 172, fat 2, fiber 3, carbs 6, protein 6

Delightful Fruity Custard

Preparation Time: 22 minutes

Serves: 6
Nutrition Values
- Calories:- 517
- Carbohydrate:- 80.3g
- Protein:- 15.4g
- Fat:- 15.9g
- Sugar:- 60.5g
- Sodium:- 0.36g

Ingredients
- 1 lb. sponge cake; sliced
- 4 cups milk
- 6 eggs
- ¾ cup sugar
- 1 tsp. vanilla extract
- Round stainless-steel pan
- 1/4 tsp. ground cinnamon
- 1 cup whipped cream
- Fresh fruits; sliced
- 1 cup homemade fruit jelly
- 1 pinch sea salt

Directions:
1. Beat milk, eggs, sugar, cinnamon, vanilla extract and salt in the bowl until they become smooth.
2. Transfer the mixture to the steel pan.
3. Pour a cup of water into Instant Pot and place the trivet inside,
4. Cover the bowl with tin foil, poke some holes in it then place it over the trivet.
5. Secure the lid and cook on manual for 7 minutes at high pressure,
6. When it beeps; do a quick release and remove the lid.
7. In a serving bowl add a thin layer of sponge cake then the custard, fruits and cream on top.
8. Garnish with jelly cubes and refrigerate overnight. Serve and enjoy.

Sweet Honey Yogurt Recipe

Preparation Time: 9 hours 15 minutes

Serves: 6
Nutrition Values
- Calories:- 383
- Carbohydrate:- 44.4g
- Protein:- 22.5g
- Fat:- 13.6g
- Sugar:- 41.6g
- Sodium:- 0.31g

Ingredients
- 1/4 cup honey
- 1-gallon milk
- 1 tbsp. vanilla extract
- ⅓ cup Greek yoghurt
- Cheesecloth
- Wire sieve

Directions:
1. Add the milk to Instant Pot and lock the lid.
2. Boil on the *yogurt function* for 1 hour. Remove the lid after the beep.
3. Stir in Greek yoghurt, honey and vanilla extract then secure the lid.
4. Press the yogurt key and adjust the time to 8 hours,
5. When it beeps; do a natural release then remove the lid.
6. Place the wire sieve in a bowl layer it with cheesecloth.
7. Pour the prepared curd into the bowl and strain the excess liquid.
8. Let it strain for 45 minutes then remove the thick yoghurt. Serve or store for later use.

IP Brown Fudge Cake

Preparation Time: 12 minutes

Serves: 4
Nutrition Values
- Calories:- 166
- Carbohydrate:- 21.2g
- Protein:- 3g
- Fat:- 8.7g
- Sugar:- 13.9g
- Sodium:- 28mg

Ingredients
- 2 tsp. fresh orange zest; grated finely
- 1/4 cup milk
- 3 ramekins
- 2 tbsp. extra-virgin olive oil
- Powdered sugar; as required
- 1 egg
- 1/4 cup all-purpose flour
- 1/4 cup sugar
- 1 tbsp. cocoa powder
- 1/2 tsp. baking powder

Directions:
1. Add all the Ingredients to a large bowl except powdered sugar.

2. Whisk all the Ingredients well to prepare a smooth mixture,
3. Grease the three ramekins and pour the prepared mixture into the ramekins,
4. Pour a cup of water into Instant Pot. Place the steamer trivet inside,
5. Arrange the ramekins over the trivet.
6. Secure the lid and cook on manual for 6 minutes at high pressure,
7. When it beeps; do a quick release and remove the lid.
8. Let the ramekins cool. Sprinkle powdered sugar on top of each cake, Serve,

Awesome Apple Bread Pudding

Preparation Time: 85 minutes

Serves: 8
Nutrition Values
- Calories:- 554
- Carbohydrate:- 95.4g
- Protein:- 5.1g
- Fat:- 18.5g
- Sugar:- 67g
- Sodium:- 0.23g

Ingredients
- 3 cups apples peeled; cored and cubed
- 1 cup sugar
- 2 cups flour
- 1 tbsp. baking powder
- 2 eggs
- 1 tbsp. vanilla
- 1 tbsp. apple pie spice

Topping:
- 1 stick butter
- 2 cups brown sugar
- 1 cup heavy cream

Directions:
1. Combine flour and baking powder in a bowl and set aside,
2. Mix butter, eggs sugar and apple pie spice with the electric mixer.
3. Add all the dry Ingredients to the egg mixture and beat until smooth.
4. Fold in apples and pour the mixture into a 7-inch springform pan.
5. Pour a cup of water into Instant Pot and place the trivet inside,
6. Arrange the pan over the trivet. Secure the lid.
7. Cook on manual function for 70 minutes at high pressure,
8. When it beeps; do a natural release and remove the lid.
9. Boil the butter with brown sugar in a skillet over medium heat for 3 minutes,
10. Stir in cream. Mix well on low heat. Pour this mixture over the pudding and serve.

Walnut Carrot Cake

Preparation Time: 55 minutes

Serves: 4
Nutrition Values
- Calories:- 365
- Carbohydrate:- 31.2g
- Protein:- 6.8g
- Fat:- 28.1g

- Sugar:- 21.5g
- Sodium:- 0.28g

Ingredients
- 1/4 cup walnuts chopped.
- 1 ½ eggs
- 1/2 cup almond flour
- ⅓ cup Swerve
- 1/2 tsp. baking powder
- ¾ tsp. apple pie spice
- 2 tbsp. coconut oil
- 1/4 cup heavy whipping cream
- 1/2 cup carrots shredded

Directions:
1. Beat the eggs, oil, cream, swerve, four and apple spice in a bowl
2. Stir in carrots and walnuts,
3. Transfer the mixture to a greased 6-inch springform pan. Cover with tin foil.
4. Pour a cup of water into Instant Pot and place the trivet inside,
5. Set the pan on the trivet and secure the lid.
6. Cook on manual for 40 minutes at high pressure,
7. When it beeps; do a natural release and remove the lid. Allow it to cool and serve.

Instant Chocolate Crème Brûlée

Preparation Time: 23 minutes

Serves: 4
Nutrition Values
- Calories:- 386
- Carbohydrate:- 29g
- Protein:- 4.8g
- Fat:- 28.3g
- Sugar:- 26.3g
- Sodium:- 35mg

Ingredients
- 4 ramekins
- 1/4 cup superfine sugar
- 1/2 tbsp. grated chocolate
- 5 egg yolks
- 2 cups heavy cream
- 1 tbsp. vanilla extract
- 1/2 tbsp. cocoa powder
- 1/2 cup sugar

Directions:
1. Beat the egg yolks, cream, cocoa powder, vanilla extract and sugar in a large bowl.
2. Divide the mixture into 4 ramekins,
3. Pour a cup of water into Instant Pot and place the trivet inside,
4. Arrange the ramekins over the trivet.
5. Secure the lid and cook on manual function for 13 minutes at high pressure,
6. When it beeps; do a quick release and remove the lid.
7. Let the ramekin cool and refrigerate for 4 hours, Sprinkle superfine sugar and grated chocolate on top and serve.

Awesome Wine Glazed Apples

Preparation Time: 15 minutes

Serves: 4
Nutrition Values
- Calories:- 227
- Carbohydrate:- 51.4g
- Protein:- 0.9g
- Fat:- 0.5g
- Sugar:- 40.6gg
- Sodium:- 10mg

Ingredients
- 4 apples; cored
- 3/4 cup red wine
- ⅓ cup demerara sugar
- 1/4 cup raisins
- 3/4 tsp. ground cinnamon

Directions:
1. Add all the Ingredients to Instant Pot.
2. Secure the lid. Cook on manual function for 10 minutes at high pressure,
3. When it beeps; do a quick release and remove the lid. Top the apples with some cooking oil and serve.

Yummy Apple Custard Trifle

Preparation Time: 27 minutes

Serves: 4
Nutrition Values
- Calories:- 375
- Carbohydrate:- 54.1g
- Protein:- 16.4g
- Fat:- 11.6g
- Sugar:- 52g
- Sodium:- 0.26g

Ingredients
- 4 cups milk
- 6 eggs
- 4 tbsp. sugar
- 2 tbsp. water
- 1 medium apple thinly sliced
- ¾ cup sugar
- 1 tsp. vanilla extract
- 1/4 tsp. ground cinnamon
- Round stainless-steel pan
- 1 pinch sea salt

Directions:
1. Beat the milk, eggs, sugar, cinnamon, vanilla extract and salt in the bowl until they become smooth.
2. Transfer the mixture to the steel pan.
3. Pour a cup of water into Instant Pot and place the trivet inside,
4. Cover the bowl with tin foil, poke some holes in it then place it over the trivet.
5. Secure the lid and cook on manual for 7 minutes at high pressure,

6. When it beeps; do a quick release and remove the lid.
7. Transfer the custard to the serving bowl and cover the top with apple slices,
8. Boil the sugar with 2 tbsp. of water in the skillet and let it caramelize, Glaze the top of custard apples with this mixture and serve when cool.

Almond Cheese-cake

Preparation Time: 28 minutes

Serves: 4
Nutrition Values
- Calories:- 248
- Carbohydrate:- 11g
- Protein:- 7.6g
- Fat:- 24g
- Sugar:- 8g
- Sodium:- 190mg

Ingredients
- 1/4 cup almonds; thinly sliced
- 1/4 cup powdered sugar
- 1 egg
- 8 oz. cream cheese softened
- 1 tbsp. powdered peanut butter
- 1/2 tsp. pure vanilla extract

Directions:
1. Blend the eggs and cream cheese in a blender to form a smooth mixture,
2. Add the brown sugar, peanut butter and vanilla extract to the egg mixture and blend.
3. Transfer the mixture to a greased ramekin.
4. Pour water into Instant Pot and place the trivet inside,
5. Arrange the ramekin over the trivet.
6. Secure the lid and cook on manual function for 18 minutes at high pressure,
7. When it beeps; do a quick release and remove the lid.
8. Let the ramekin cool and top it with almonds, Refrigerate the cake for 8 hours, Serve,

Conclusion

Thanks for purchasing this book. It's my firm belief that it will provide you with all the answers to your questions.

Made in the USA
San Bernardino, CA
24 August 2019